1986

SWAZILAND

PROFILES · NATIONS OF CONTEMPORARY AFRICA
Larry W. Bowman, Series Editor

Mozambique: From Colonialism to Revolution, 1900—1982,
Allen Isaacman and Barbara Isaacman

Senegal: An African Nation Between Islam and the West,
Sheldon Gellar

The Seychelles: Unquiet Islands, Marcus Franda

Swaziland: Tradition and Change in a Southern African Kingdom,
Alan R. Booth

Tanzania: An African Experiment, Rodger Yeager

The Comoro Islands, Malyn Newitt

Ghana, Deborah Pellow and Naomi Chazan

Ivory Coast, Barbara C. Lewis

Kenya, Norman N. Miller

Niger, Robert B. Charlick and James T. Thomson

Nigeria, Timothy M. Shaw and Orobola Fasehun

Also of Interest

Nigeria in Search of a Stable Civil-Military System,
J. 'Bayo Adekson

SWAZILAND
Tradition and Change in a Southern African Kingdom

Alan R. Booth

Westview Press • Boulder, Colorado

Gower • Hampshire, England

Profiles / Nations of Contemporary Africa

Jacket photos (*clockwise from upper left*): Swazi man combining in his dress the traditional and the modern; Usutu Pulp Company Ltd. mill and timberland; a roadside food market; a Swazi homestead near Mahlanya. All photos by the author.

Copyright © 1983 by Westview Press, Inc.

Published in 1983 in the United States of America by
  Westview Press, Inc.
  5500 Central Avenue
  Boulder, Colorado 80301
  Frederick A. Praeger, President and Publisher

Published in 1983 in Great Britain by
  Gower Publishing Company Limited
  Gower House, Croft Road
  Aldershot, Hampshire GU11 3HR, England

Library of Congress Cataloging in Publication Data
Booth, Alan R.
  Swaziland: tradition and change in a southern African
  kingdom.
  (Profiles. Nations of contemporary Africa)
  Bibliography: p.
  1. Swaziland. I. Title. II. Series.
DT971.B58 1983   968.1'3   83-6511
ISBN 0-86531-233-8

British Library Cataloguing in Publication Data
Booth, Alan
  Swaziland: tradition and change in a southern
  African kingdom.—(Africa profile)
  1. Swaziland—History
  I. Title II. Series
968.13   DT961
ISBN 0-566-00553-0

Printed and bound in the United States of America

For my students
at the University College of Swaziland, 1980–1981

*If a free society cannot help the many who
are poor, it cannot save the few who are rich.*
—President John F. Kennedy
Inaugural Address, January 20, 1961

Contents

Illustrations

Tables

Acknowledgments

I spent the academic year 1980-1981 as Fulbright lecturer at the University College of Swaziland and at the same time conducted research under the auspices of the American Philosophical Society. Subsequent research trips have been sponsored by the Office of Research and Sponsored Programs, and the Baker Awards Committee, at Ohio University. All of these I acknowledge with gratitude.

Julius Dlamini, director of the National Archives, and Esther Nxumalo, librarian at the Ministry of Economic Planning and Statistics, were most attentive to all my needs and requests. Derek Cottrill and Peter Talbot of The Employment Bureau of Africa made their papers and statistics readily available.

I am indebted as well to a number of people in Swaziland, of various backgrounds and persuasions, whose insights are reflected in this volume. Among them are Philip Bonner, Jonathan Crush, John Daniel, Fion de Vletter, Maboya Fakudze, Thoko Ginindza, Nathan Kirsh, Stanley Mabizela, Pica Magagula, John McSeveney, Randall Packard, Robert Stephens, and Daniel Swanson. John Daniel and Fion de Vletter commented on an early draft. Any errors that remain are, however, mine.

Alan R. Booth

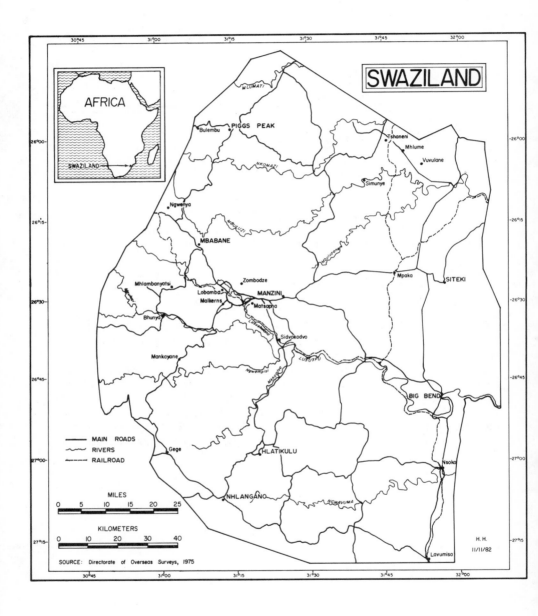

SWAZILAND

AFRICA

SWAZILAND →

MLUMATI

Bulembu PIGGS PEAK

Tshaneni
Mhlume
Vuvulane

NKOMAZI

Simunye

Ngwenya

MBULUZI

MBABANE

MBULUZANE

Mpaka SITEKI

Mhlambanyatsi

Zombodze

Lobamba MANZINI

Malkerns Matsapha

MLUMENI

Bhunya

Sidvokodvo

LUSUTU

Mankayane

Ngwempisi

MKHONDO

BIG BEND

MAIN ROADS
RIVERS
RAILROAD

Gege

HLATIKULU

Nsoka

MILES

0   5   10   15   20   25

NHLANGANO

NGWAVUMA

KILOMETERS

0   10   20   30   40

H. H.
11/11/82

Lavumisa

SOURCE: Directorate of Overseas Surveys, 1975

Introduction

Swaziland is a small kingdom situated in southeastern Africa, lying between the Republic of South Africa and Mozambique. Although the area it occupies is modest (slightly larger than the state of Connecticut), it is strategically located in a region of great conflict. That, and its wealth of natural resources, make it far more important in the subcontinent than its size would indicate.

Swaziland's position in the region has always had a central effect on its history. It lay across the major migration route of Bantu speakers from central into southern Africa in prehistoric times; these migrants were the ancestors of Swaziland's present population. In the early nineteenth century the wave of movement was reversed, and Swaziland was forced to defend itself against the threat of invasion from the south in the aftermath of the Zulu wars of expansion. At the end of that century the threat came from the west, as the Transvaal's ambitions for access to the sea and the Europeans' appetites for Swaziland's resources turned the country into a pawn in the "scramble for Africa" and eventually into a British protectorate.

In the 1980s Swaziland must look to all four compass points in attending to its future. From the north and east, the African National Congress (ANC) uses Swaziland as an infiltration route from Mozambique into South Africa. To the east and west Swaziland seeks more land and to the east, access to the sea, a prospect being held out to it by South Africa in return for considerations as yet unspecified. To the south, Swaziland's historic enemies, the Zulus, warn that if that happens at their expense, blood will flow.

So it may come as a surprise to the casual reader to learn that Swaziland is essentially a peaceful and conservative country whose people, for all their proud military tradition, for the most part quietly pursue the good life. A major theme of modern Swazi history, this reader will discover, is the efforts of the government and the citizenry to deal peaceably and

1

Mbabane, 1908 and 1983 (*opposite page*). 1908 photo from the Swaziland National Archives; 1983 photo by the author.

wisely with the facts of their geographic position and abundance of resources and the greed that those resources have excited in others.

In truth, Swaziland is an extraordinarily rich and beautiful country. Parts of it are as lush and well watered as any in the world, and beneath the ground lies a wealth of certain minerals. Soil fertility was the basis for early Swazi prosperity in grain and cattle, and that prosperity was what first excited the attention of the Europeans, the pastoral farmers of the eastern Transvaal. Boers were followed by British prospectors seeking their fortunes in gold and tin in the 1880s, and the rush for concessions changed the complexion of Swaziland forever.

The agrarian cornucopia that Swaziland has become in this century was largely the result of the European expropriation of the better lands after the Boer War and application of water engineering to them. The latter undertaking was a post–World War II phenomenon that resulted in Swaziland's abundance of sugar, citrus fruit, and other export crops grown in irrigated fields. Commercial forestry was also launched by Europeans on Swazi-forfeited land after World War II, and timber became the kingdom's largest export earner after sugar. Exploitation of minerals—asbestos, iron, and coal—was also foreign controlled.

Agricultural and mining investment was followed in the 1970s by large-scale capitalization of light manufacturing and service (mainly tourist)

industries, the result of an aggressive government policy to establish a commercial base for the economy. Parastatal corporations were established and a tax policy formulated to make such investments attractive, and they have been very successful. In 1977 Swaziland's per capita gross domestic product (GDP) stood at E 404 ($580) per annum,[1] placing the kingdom twelfth in the World Bank ranking of fifty-four African countries.

But not everyone is rich. In fact Swaziland is not much better off than most Third World countries in its attempts to industrialize and become commercially successful in the world marketplace. International capital invests where it finds cheap labor and investment concessions. Swaziland, in responding to those market forces, had by the early 1980s paid a heavy price in terms of an economy heavily dependent on foreign capital and a badly skewed income distribution.

Data on incomes are inadequate, but those available point to the conclusion (as outlined in a 1977 International Labor Office study) that "despite [Swaziland's] apparent prosperity, poverty affects a large proportion of the population." Rural Swazi income, it reckoned, ran to about E 53 per year; urban area income was closer to E 506. Non-Swazis averaged E 1,782 per year. Unemployment, which two decades previously had been largely unknown, by the late 1970s had reached a level (particularly among the educated) at which governments begin to worry about social stability. Finally, amidst the agricultural abundance, the report concluded, "The proportion of families not able to satisfy the minimum required levels of nutrition were in the neighborhood of 44 per cent in urban areas and 65 per cent in rural areas. The income of an average household falls short of the minimum amount needed to meet its basic needs by about 33 per cent in rural and about 12 per cent in urban areas."[2]

Much of this book deals with the causes of these imbalances and their details and investigates some of the alternatives open to the new generation of Swazi leadership now coming to power. In neither its findings nor its conclusions does it make a claim to objectivity; few, on the other hand, will find it doctrinaire. Either position would be a disservice to the reader. But the heat of the debate over the condition of the Third World and its causes and remedies effectively invalidates the middle of the road position in any account such as this. The point of view that informs these pages is that, put simply, there is an economic basis to the scheme of things, and one ought to remember that—although not that alone—when reconstructing the past or describing the present. And one ought to be able to heed the historian Geoffrey Barraclough's warnings against the "obsession with causality" and "neurotic absorption in questions in motivation"[3] while still recognizing that people and nations have interests to promote and that history is made when they act on them.

The pages that follow draw liberally from what is known as "underdevelopment theory" in their assessment of the past hundred years. That thesis applied to Africa sees the colonial period as the incorporation of peripheral societies into a burgeoning world capitalist economy whose need for expansion began to touch the continent (which had previously experienced only unequal trade, slave trade, and plunder) in the mid-nineteenth century. The goal of the colonial powers, the extraction of surplus from the peripheral countries for the benefit of the metropoles, had previously been carried out by armed enforcement of trade disparities, which had been far more cost effective than actual occupation. But when, in time, European rivalries in Africa necessitated such occupation, the enormous costs involved demanded that the exploitation of the colonized be legitimized and enforced. Systems were devised, based commonly on taxation and the expropriation of land, that delivered up capital's requirements—forced labor, enforcement of contracts and property rights, and so on—all previously unknown in the newly colonized societies.

During the 1880s the discovery of vast quantities of gold in South Africa made it a classic theater for regional underdevelopment. This was true in part because low-quality and deeply embedded ore made gold mining easily the most capital- and labor-intensive of all industries. The generation and reproduction of a cheap and reliable labor force thus became a cardinal basis for British colonial policy in all of southern Africa, including Swaziland. The architect of that policy, Sir Alfred Milner (high commissioner for South Africa from 1897 to 1905), worked from a vision of "a self-governing white community . . . supported by a well-treated and justly governed black labour force from Cape Town to Zambezi."[4] How that policy—stripped of its Kiplingesque rhetoric—affected Swazi society thenceforward is described herein.

Dependency theory, companion to the concept of underdevelopment, holds that when the high costs of colonial rule dictated that the rulers withdraw after World War II, they left in power a class in whose interest it was to perpetuate those exploitative ties with metropolitan capital. Questions of neocolonialism, and the nature of its contemporary application to Swaziland, are also discussed here.

The death in 1982 of Ngwenyama (King) Sobhuza II, who was born before the Boer War and who had ruled Swaziland for over sixty years, marked the end of an era in the kingdom. During his lifetime Swaziland had entered into the colonial era and (thanks in no small part to him) emerged from it with its sovereignty intact. Sobhuza was a remarkable historical figure—surely the greatest of the Swazi kings. He was both a fervent traditionalist and an authentic revolutionary. When he could not outwit his colonial masters he outlasted them, and he survived the colonial period with his people preserved and his own powers immeasurably greater than those he had inherited. And in an age when kings everywhere came toppling down, Sobhuza not only endured but reigned supreme—not so much by the force of arms or money as by the genuine love of his people. His skills as a politician, a diplomat, an entrepreneur, and a humanitarian are already legendary. The character of Swaziland today is deeply reflective of that of the man who ruled it for six decades.

But by the time of his death, certain aspects of that national character had become sources of concern in many quarters. A parastatal fund (the Tibiyo Taka Ngwane Fund) and its infrastructure, by which the king had capitalized the monarchy with such success, had so entwined themselves with foreign capital as to raise the question of who controlled whom. Moreover, as his life ebbed away, the *ngwenyama* harkened during the final months to the voices of traditionalism, which had always been strong, and agreed to a land deal with Pretoria that involved potentially the transfer of 2,000,000 acres (800,000 hectares [ha]) known as KaNgwane and more than three-quarters of a million people from South Africa to the kingdom. Swazi kings had once ruled over many of the lands in question, but aside from the satisfaction of those nationalist sentiments it was difficult for many to see what benefits could be derived to balance the damage the scheme was likely to inflict. For in readjusting historical borders and in forcibly denationalizing so many South African Swazis (which Pretoria insisted on as part of the deal), the scheme was likely to place Swaziland before the world as a flouter of Organization of African Unity (OAU) principle, a furtherer of apartheid, and (in effect) a charter member of a "Constellation of States" dominated by South Africa. That appeared to be a heavy price to pay for tradition.

By late 1982 the procedures for the succession, unused for over eighty years, had produced a new king. Much turned on the wisdom of the choice. For the world that the youthful Prince Makhosetive faced in 1983 was far different from the one the infant Sobhuza had confronted in 1899. That world had been bad enough; for Sobhuza had inherited a kingdom beset by the avarice of foreign adventurers and statesmen, one that previously, under two misguided kings, had lost for a time its independence, its lands, and seemingly its will. Sobhuza spent a lifetime regaining them all, and (with the exception of the land) he had done so in brilliant fashion. The new king would have to deal with foreign ambitions far stronger yet immeasurably more subversive, while caught in the maelstrom of a human rights struggle in the region that allowed for neither peace nor neutrality.

Yet history has always provided the Swazi with decisive leadership in their most challenging times. With such leadership, and with some good fortune, Swaziland stands a good chance of fulfilling the needs and aspirations of its people. This book will provide some insights into the nature of those needs and aspirations and the ways they can be fulfilled.

1

History of the Swazi Kingdom to 1963

The Swazi are a Bantu-speaking people inhabiting a small, strategically located country in southeastern Africa.[1] They are predominantly Nguni in language and culture, although their early admixture with the Sotho, who now inhabit mainly the Transvaal and the Orange Free State, and to a lesser extent, the Tsonga, whose home is now Mozambique, has left them with cultural traces of these peoples.

Tradition has it that the Swazi, as part of the Nguni expansion southward from east-central Africa, crossed the Limpopo River and settled in southern Tsongaland (Mozambique) in the late fifteenth century. Their leader was Dlamini, a man of Embo Nguni background. Other Nguni-speakers akin to the Swazi, notably the Xhosa and the Zulu, migrated further south, the Zulu settling neighboring areas of what is now north-central Natal. But the Swazi, led by Dlamini's descendants, remained for over two hundred years in what is now southern Mozambique, in the region of Maputo.

THE FORMATIVE YEARS: NGWANE III AND HIS SUCCESSORS (1750–1839)

The original inhabitants of modern Swaziland, the San, had by the sixteenth century given way to the Sotho. Not until about 1750 did the Swazi challenge Sotho primacy there. Then, for reasons still not clear, King Ngwane III (d. 1780) led his Swazi followers across the Lubombo Mountains and settled on the northern bank of the Pongola River, not far from present-day Nhlangano in southern Swaziland. There he built his capital, Lobamba, which is still celebrated as the birthplace of the nation and the wellspring of the "true Swazi." Those who trace their lineage back to this small group of Ngwane's followers call themselves *bakaNgwane*, "the people of Ngwane," and often refer to their nation as *kaNgwane*, "the country of Ngwane."

Ngwane's son Ndvungunya (d. 1815) and grandson Sobhuza I (d. 1839) ruled in dangerous times. This was the era of the *mfecane*, the "time of crushing," during which new nations were forged out of the remains of old societies uprooted during the Zulu wars of expansion. Great figures emerged as leaders contemporary with Ndvungunya and Sobhuza: Dingiswayo of the Mathetwa, Zwide of the Ndwandwe, Moshoeshoe of the Basotho, Mzilikazi of the Ndebele, Soshangane of the Gaza, and Shaka, the formidable Zulu king. State formation by peaceable means and migration without bloodshed were things of the past. The chiefs who prevailed were all men of ambition and of violence, and so it was with the Swazi kings. Tales are still told of the tyranny of Ndvungunya and Sobhuza; the royal administrative capital became known as Eshishelweni, "the place of burning," suggestive of violent conquest. It was Ndvungunya who formed the beginnings of the Swazi army and Sobhuza who used it with notable success in conquering and absorbing neighboring peoples, Nguni and Sotho. Sobhuza came to be known to his followers as Somhlohlo, "the wonder."

The predominant force south of the Pongola during Sobhuza's time was the Ndwandwe, led by the formidable Zwide. He was then at the height of his power, and Sobhuza was, for all his prowess, a realist. His people, especially his army, were no match for Zwide's when it came to numbers, and so when a quarrel arose over some fertile garden lands in the Pongola Valley, Sobhuza led his people north rather than face sure annihilation from a Ndwandwe attack.

The push north, which was slow but not without violence, kept to the western mountains to avoid the disease-ridden lowlands, where the scourge of man was malaria and of beast, trypanosomiasis. Then, as now, Swazi men counted their wealth in their women and children and their cattle. Most of the migrants were men of the Dlamini clan and their wives, but there were others, some of them not of Embo Nguni stock, who had given their allegiance to the monarchy at Eshishelweni and cast their lot with Sobhuza on the move north. They include some clan names prominent in present-day Swaziland: Mhlanga, Hlope, Fakudze, Simelane, Matsebula, and still others, who became known as *Bemdzabuko*, "true Swazi."

West-central Swaziland, into which the Sobhuza party pushed, was occupied by loosely organized groups of Nguni and Sotho, from whom the king demanded allegiance. Those who submitted and paid tribute were allowed to retain the trappings of independence, including their hereditary chiefs. Those who resisted were destroyed and the survivors incorporated. That group of clans which retained their identity (among them Maseko, Gama, Magagula, Motsa, Gwebu, and other names prominent today) became known as *Emakhandzambili*, "those found ahead." Sobhuza eventually established his presence in the region of the Mdzimba Mountains, which afforded defensible caves in time of attack. At their base, in about 1820, he built his new headquarters, Lobamba.[2] The royal homestead was named Elangeni, "in the sun," which became the administrative center of the kingdom.

Thus was Dlamini power established in central Swaziland. Once the king's position was stabilized, Sobhuza's armies ranged further afield to the north, conquering tribes and thereby increasing both the number of subjects and his forces. Even the Pedi, deep in the Transvaal interior, were not immune to his attacks.

Sobhuza's power should not be viewed as absolute or unquestioned. Like all the great figures who prevailed during those troubled times, he did so by a successful mixing of force, political skill, diplomacy, guile, and bluster. Sobhuza, like Moshoeshoe, migrated until he found a mountain redoubt for his people; like Moshoeshoe, he used statecraft in combination with force to achieve his aims; like Moshoeshoe, he sometimes chose not to fight. He continued to avoid conflict with the Ndwandwe and others more powerful than he. Instead, he took a daughter of Zwide as his principal wife, and he sent two of his own daughters to the Zulu king, Shaka.[3] Indeed, the Swazi king is said to have paid Shaka a state visit and to have been warmly received. But in 1828 no diplomatic skills were able to stop Dingane, Shaka's brother, murderer, and successor, from marching his armies into Swaziland, and on that occasion Sobhuza took to the hills and the caves. Only at the end of his life did Sobhuza deem it prudent to stand in the face of a Zulu invasion, when in 1838 he took on an attacking force of Dingane's army—then dispirited by its defeat at the hands of the Boers at Blood River—and sent it reeling in defeat.[4]

Sobhuza's grip on Swaziland was, in fact, tenuous. His kingdom resembled, in Philip Bonner's words, "more closely an army of occupation camped out in hostile territory than a settled administration." Little of the land he conquered was in fact settled, the bulk of the population being clustered under the protection of scattered military towns. Only in Sobhuza's final years did an administrative presence and a nascent sense of security begin to underpin Swazi society.[5]

MSWATI AND HIS SUCCESSORS (1839–1875)

Sobhuza's legacy to his successor was a country far larger, stronger, and more populous than the one he had inherited. His followers numbered several thousands, not hundreds. He claimed to rule as far as modern-day Barberton in the north, Carolina in the west, the Pongola in the south, and the Lubombo range in the east.

His successor was Mswati (d. 1865), surely the fiercest, and some say the greatest, of Swaziland's fighting kings.[6] In part those qualities stemmed from the disputed nature of the succession, which finally involved a pitched battle between the forces of the youthful pretender and those of an adult half-brother and would-be usurper, who perished with many of his men. Consequently the young Mswati and his mother were installed in their royal positions before either of them was properly prepared. Such circumstances during his formative years would have predisposed him to act with the fierceness and decisiveness that came to mark his later reign.

The quarter century of Mswati's reign was a critical period in Swazi state formation in several ways. Historians have always acknowledged Mswati's military prowess, which produced a greatly expanded and more securely defended state by the time of his death in 1865. His crack regiments were used both locally, against the stubborn autonomy of several *Emakhandzambili* chiefs, and abroad. From Hoho in northern Swaziland and from bases further forward, the king deployed his regiments into the Transvaal until they ranged into what is now Zimbabwe. To the east, he used his power to dabble in the politics of succession in the Gaza kingdom, east of the Lubombo range. All the while, during the first two decades of his reign, Mswati was forced to deal with successive rebellions by two of his elder brothers and to repel a like number of determined Zulu attacks.

The key objectives in all of this maneuvering were cattle, captives, and suzerainty rather than the acquisition of new lands. Mswati defended his lands resolutely against the Zulus, but he did not chase them in their retreat. He punished the Pedi in the north for their transgressions, then withdrew. He tried to influence politics in Gazaland, and he decisively established his paramountcy among the *Emakhandzambili*. Finally, he settled conquered groups, placed chiefs over others, and gave asylum to still others (including the unsuccessful pretenders to the Gaza throne) to the extent that a third element among the Swazi came to be identifiable as *Emafikamuva*, "those who came late." They included such families as Nkambule, Hlatswhakho, Dladla, Masuko, Nxumalo, and Vilakati.[7]

Such formidable accomplishments presumed an enhanced basis for the king's authority, both military and political. Mswati achieved this basis by recasting Swazi society and by instituting new measures that both practically and ritually centralized his authority and strengthened Dlamini legitimacy. Until his time, the army had been decentralized, each chief being responsible for mobilizing local warriors on Lobamba's command. Now, influenced by his mother, Thandile laZwide,[8] Mswati adopted the Ndwandwe institution of nationwide age regiments, cutting across local boundaries and kinship loyalties to focus loyalty on the king.[9] Thenceforward Swazi youth were conscripted and regimented by orders direct from the capital. Mobilization was facilitated (and administrative control enforced) by the establishment of a network of royal villages throughout the kingdom. It was at this time that the Swazi renown for military prowess and rigid discipline really began.

Ritual innovation accompanied this centralization. The *Incwala* ("first fruits") ceremony came to focus national attention at each harvest specifically on the king and on his special powers to bring forth rain and abundant crops. Rituals imported from the Ndwandwe reinforced this legitimacy.[10]

It was during Mswati's reign that we can identify the beginnings of Swazi class formation, including the class basis for the reproduction of the monarchy. The age-regiment system became a means for royal extraction of surplus from the peasantry; youth were now withdrawn from the agricultural cycle of the homestead and set to work in the king's fields.

War booty—cattle and captives—were retained by the king, portions being redistributed to war heroes and those otherwise favored. Stores of wealth in the forms of cattle and women gradually accrued to the royal house through a system of differential *lobola* (roughly, "bridewealth"), whereby a princess commanded a premium of cattle in marriage, while the king claimed the right of seizure over any maiden he fancied. Customarily, marriage within the ruling clan was preferred. Royal fines were exacted in cattle, and access to the best pasturage (in fact, to all land) was controlled by the king. In this manner, wealth and power became further concentrated in the hands of the royal house and the Dlamini clan. Beyond the inner circle, loyalty to the monarchy—as exhibited by the contribution of tribute labor or by bravery in war that enriched the royal herds and harem—came to be associated with upward mobility.[11]

The final years of Mswati's reign witnessed the coalescing of these class forces and military might. The Dlaminis strengthened their authority over peoples of the realm, and their armies extended their sway over neighboring tribes until the Swazi became "one of the most powerful peoples in Southern Africa."[12]

But that influence did not last for long. Mswati's death brought on a ten-year period of dissension and turmoil centering on a dispute over the succession. An older brother took up arms against the council's choice of Mswati's minor son, Ludvonga (d. 1872). When Ludvonga died, suddenly and mysteriously, the council decreed the execution of his suspected murderer, the prince regent. That, in turn, sparked off a period of intrigue and armed conflict between rival elder brothers, which divided the army and sapped its strength. Finally, influenced by the queen mother, the venerable Thandile, the nation agreed to accept a compromise candidate, the quiet and motherless Mbandzeni (d. 1889). Chosen as king "less for his exceptional qualities than for his exceptional lack of them," Mbandzeni was duly installed in mid-1875.[13] As subsequent events proved, it was far from a felicitous choice.

MBANDZENI: CONCESSIONS AND FOREIGN INTRIGUES (1875–1889)

The Boers of the eastern Transvaal, whose longstanding covetousness of lush Swazi pastures had been kept in check by their respect for Mswati's armies, were quick to seize the advantage presented by this interregnum. Previously their intercourse with the Swazi had been cooperative and profitable, but circumspect. For years the Transvaalers had purchased Swazi war captives, even children, for labor. In 1845 Mswati had ceded to the Transvaal Boers a large piece of territory in the southwest, inhabited by vassal Sotho and astride the historic invasion route of the Zulus—the same region in which he had authorized the settlement of the first Wesleyan missionaries the year before. Ten years later, another large area had been ceded to the Lydenburg Republic to the northwest, and in 1864 Mswati's regiments had assisted the Boers in suppressing some of the Lydenburg peoples. But now, in 1875, the Boers were emboldened to dabble in Swazi domestic politics for their own advantage, sending a commando numbering 400 to "assist" in Mbandzeni's coronation.

More important, rival strategic interests within the region between Boer and Briton caught the Swazis up for the first time in European diplomatic intrigues. They centered on Transvaal's access to the sea, which had been a primary ambition of its leadership since the days of the Great Trek. The realities of Portuguese control of Mozambique and British maneuvers made the most logical route appear to be through Tsongaland to Kosi Bay, the way to which lay directly through Swaziland. Boer desire for a seaport transcended the realities of their own position in the late 1870s, which was weak to the point of collapse. Militarily they were sandwiched between the danger of Sekhukhune's Pedi to the north (their campaign against the Pedi in 1876 had been a conspicuous failure) and the mounting threat of the Zulu under Cetewayo on their southern flank. Politically approaching anarchy and economically nearly bankrupt, they finally provided the British with the seeming justification for forcibly annexing the Transvaal in 1877, an act that did little to diminish either Boer nationalism or strategic ambitions.

For their part, the British were not prepared to countenance any extension of Transvaal influence in the region, most particularly in the form of independent access to the sea. Yet at the same time they were reluctant to counter Boer ambitions by extending their own jurisdiction, especially considering the resurgence of Zulu militancy, the strength of which would be demonstrated at Isandhlwana in 1879. Britain's answer to these problems was to involve the Swazi, both militarily and diplomatically, in their solution. Mbandzeni's regiments had been demonstrating their renewed prowess, raiding deep into the Lydenburg and Zoutpansberg districts. In November 1879 the British enlisted Swazi assistance in a revived campaign against Sekhukhune, on the assurance of British protection forever against the Transvaal threat to their independence. Mbandzeni, increasingly anxious about the effects of Boer pressure, agreed and dispatched a troop of 8,000 under the great general Mbovana Fakudze to bolster the British attack on the Pedi. The Swazi suffered grievous casualties, but they won the day and were thereby assured of a British guarantee of their sovereignty in perpetuity.

Consequently, when the British annexation of the Transvaal was rescinded by the Pretoria Convention of 1881, the opportunity arose to clear a debt to Mbandzeni and to finesse Boer ambitions for a seaport. A clause was inserted under which the British and Transvaal governments recognized Swaziland's independence within delineated borders. That provision was repeated in the London Convention of 1884.[14]

Yet in a way, ironically, the Pretoria and the London conventions constituted threats to the very Swazi independence they were meant to guarantee, for they rekindled Boer adventurism and boldness. The Boers became even more desirous of land, particularly the lush, year-round

European concession hunters at Mbandzeni's kraal, 1887. Photo from the Swaziland National Archives.

"sweetveld" pasturage that abounded in Swaziland. And more than ever, Swaziland after 1881 became the logical route to Kosi Bay.

Moreover, it was not just the Boers who after 1881 looked anew to Swaziland. The British did also. Minerals—gold, then tin, beginning in 1882—not grazing, drew them there. The British came as rivals of the Boers, not as protectors of Swazi interests against Boer exploitation. News of the mineral discoveries brought concessionaires by the hundreds, seeking prospecting and property rights by which to make future fortunes. The prospectors were mainly British; their zealousness and their numbers unnerved Boer grazing interests to the point that what amounted to a concessionaires' invasion by both European groups ensued. Land and mineral rights were the first to be sought; but by the end, every conceivable (and some almost inconceivable) enterprise identifiable with present or future prosperity in a developing economy was bargained for. Manufacturing, customs collection, printing and advertising, auctioneering and pawn-broking, insuring—all were licensed and monopolized. So was the right to collect the king's revenue and to grant future concessions. "Unallotted lands" and "unallotted minerals" concessions granted their holders the rights of exploitation over unassigned tracts for one hundred years. Land and mineral rights that lapsed under other concessions were to revert not to the king, but to the holders of the two "unallotted" concessions. In the history of a continent where concessioning was a dominant theme in the colonial era, the case of Swaziland was without parallel. The beguiled king and his council in the end signed away the entire country and all authority over future development. "The documents," the Swazi say, "killed us."[15]

It is too simple to say, as has been said in explanation of this tragedy, that the king was illiterate, naive, besotted. Mbandzeni was not the first Swazi king, after all, to sign away large tracts of land. Mswati had been; his motives had been wealth, diplomacy, and security. For Mbandzeni— orphaned, secluded, crowned amidst controversy and insecurity—such motives must have been all the more alluring.[16]

Whatever the motives, Mbandzeni's frenetic concessioning forever changed the character of the monarchy and the nation. For the crown, the concessions provided for the first time a formidable capital base (revenues as much as £20,000 annually by the end of the 1880s), with all the power and patronage that entailed. But such a transformation thereby made the monarchy dependent on continued access to those revenues, which would render it incapable of withstanding the future subversion of Swazi sovereignty by foreign capital. For the nation, the means of production were thereby bargained away, and with them the control of its people over their own destiny.

Certainly Mbandzeni sensed some of these dangers. As the first European settlers came, he attempted to regulate their behavior by treating them as he did any alien Africans to be incorporated. They might live and prosper on the land as long as they acknowledged the king and held to his laws. But they were not Africans, as their independent and often unruly behavior showed daily. They were not chiefs, but they behaved like chiefs, and they treated traditional authority with disdain. They came to be, in truth, a law unto themselves, moving boundary marker beacons, demanding tribute, seizing cattle, even children.

Eventually, his authority and prestige threatened, Mbandzeni requested in 1887 that the British high commissioner send a resident, only to be refused. So he turned to a familiar and profoundly trusted figure from the past, Theophilus Shepstone, who as secretary for native affairs in Natal had helped sort out Swazi entanglements with the Zulu in the past. Shepstone was asked to send a son to assist the king and council in the wiles of dealing with the whites. So came Theophilus ("Offy") Shepstone, Jr., to be resident adviser and agent of the Swazi Nation. Mbandzeni was careful to set certain limits—the king's sovereignty in all matters was spelled out, and Shepstone was both salaried and subject to dismissal— but within these, Shepstone had broad authority in all matters involving whites. Likewise, to the white Committee of Fifteen, which Shepstone established to help him govern, the king added five of his own nominees and reserved the right of veto over any decisions. In a special convocation Mbandzeni reminded the committee of his two primary concerns: that the concessioned land had not been sold to the Europeans, only leased; and that Swazi labor on that land should not be forced. Finally, the king in effect opposed to each other Boer grazing interests and British mining and development capital by granting mineral and land concessions independently.

All of these delimitations failed of their purpose, in part because any trust, however restricted, placed in Offy Shepstone was misplaced. He proved to be devious, duplicitous, and self-seeking; the bulk of the most bizarre and outrageous concessions were granted during his tenure as adviser. It was also true that during Mbandzeni's final years the lure of gold led to his abandonment of restraint, and he fixed his mark to almost any document placed before him. Allister Miller, a towering figure in the subsequent capital development of the country, described those times: "Money poured into the country. A Swazi . . . on the great path of the Concessionaires scorned any pourboir [sic] under half a crown whilst at the King's half a sovereign was the minimum. . . . Sovereigns swelled the waistbands of the Ndunas, and the Paramount Chief [Mbandzeni] handled his golden income with double hands."[17]

By the time the king died in 1889, broken in spirit and in reputation, Swaziland was overlaid with concessions, some of them competing, and in several instances overlapping three and four deep. So, too, did the interests they represented compete, British mining and trade against Boer grazing. Much of the latter was absentee except for winter, hence all the more nervous and contentious. The process of sorting out these issues soon involved their parent societies, Britain and the Transvaal, and in so doing brought a new dimension to the struggle over Swazi land and resources. Mbandzeni and his advisers bear heavy responsibility for the bargaining away of their heritage. But the events that followed went quickly beyond the ability of any Swazi to control.

THE EATING UP OF THE LAND (1889–1914)

Had the struggle among the white concessionaires taken place during an orderly transfer of power following Mbandzeni's death, things might have gone better for the Swazi. But instead a national crisis ensued. Political killings among the aristocracy over the concessions controversy had in fact predated the king's death. The continuing dispute meant that the normal tensions of the succession developed into sporadic violence. Finally, the choice of the successor went to Gwamile Mdluli (Labotsibeni, d. 1925), a woman of extraordinary wisdom and ability, as queen mother and to her eldest son, Bunu (d. 1899), as king. Gwamile's prudence and insight, which over the years were to serve her people well, were needed in full measure to check her headstrong son's behavior at times over the next decade. She was not always successful.

All the while, the concessionaires strengthened their constituencies beyond Swaziland's borders. By around 1890 there were perhaps 750 white settlers, 60 percent of whom were British. By 1893 twenty companies had been floated in Britain on the basis of the acquired concessions, capitalized at some £2 million.[18] Those numbers translated into expressions of concern about the future overseeing of the kingdom by several chambers of commerce, notably those of London, Liverpool, and Birmingham. That concern centered on an increasingly obvious local Boer interest, shared by Pretoria, in annexing Swaziland. That interest reflected a Boer realization that most of the grazing concessions were for only eight years, and thus needed to be secured, and that the Transvaal's hope of access to the sea presupposed its domination of Swaziland. Pretoria (now the South African Republic) had consequently acquired for itself since 1887 those concessions that were essentially the powers of government: customs and licenses, railroads and telegraphs, postal and survey services, even the right to collect all revenues for the king (the Private Revenue Concession, which obliged Pretoria to pay the king the first £12,000 collected annually).[19]

These conflicting interests led both London and Pretoria to strike a compromise, to which Queen Regent Gwamile (Bunu being still a minor) assented. The Convention of 1890 once again guaranteed Swazi independence and established a provisional government to replace the discredited white committee. It also set up a special court that was to adjudicate all disputes involving Europeans and to undertake a judicial enquiry into the validity of all disputed concessions.[20]

The court validated the great bulk of the concessions, but the 1890 Convention itself (including the provisional government) lasted scarcely three years. Altered strategic considerations were largely responsible for its termination. The discovery of gold on the Witwatersrand in 1886 had by the early 1890s created the means for the Transvaal government under Paul Kruger to launch initiatives, rather than react to them. Its main external objectives, territorial expansion and diplomatic support outside the British orbit, placed renewed emphasis on access to the sea. Mineral discoveries had also led to the rise of Cecil Rhodes, by then Cape prime minister and Kruger's arch-rival in each of his expansionist aims. Rhodes's main concern by the 1890s was a free hand for Britain to the north in what subsequently became Rhodesia, and to secure that he was prepared to trade access to the sea, through Swaziland, to Kruger. That became the essence of the deal that was struck. In 1893 and 1894 negotiations between Britain and the Transvaal culminated by making Swaziland a "political dependency" of the Transvaal in the third Swaziland Convention of 1894.

An organic proclamation to that effect was presented to the Swazi queen regent for her assent and, upon her refusal to endorse it, was included without her signature in the 1894 convention. Thus were the successive British guarantees of Swazi independence (1881, 1884, and 1890) traded away in return for Rhodes's free access to Central Africa.

It was during the succeeding period of Transvaal administration (1895–1899) that the Swazi first experienced the impact of economic deprivation. Part was caused by nature, part by man. Rinderpest struck and decimated the cattle herds, beginning in 1894. In 1898 began the collection of tax, with the dual aim of extracting surplus to fund Boer administration and of providing induced wage labor (the tax was payable in cash) for local capital and for the gold mines on the Witwatersrand in the Transvaal.

Any Swazi illusions about their sovereignty that lingered after the imposition of the tax were dispelled that same year by an incident involving the newly installed young king, Bunu. A leading councillor, Mbaba Sibandze, was executed for witchcraft, and the king, who had been implicated, fled to Zululand rather than submit to the court jurisdiction of the Transvaal. The Boers sought to seize this opportunity to rid themselves of the king. But the British, who were represented by a consul in Swaziland, were more foresighted as to the advantages of preserving at least the appearance of an independent monarchy. So, with suitable assurances exchanged, a trial of sorts was held, the king was fined and reinstated, and thenceforth the legal jurisdictional powers of the monarchy were severely circumscribed.

The outbreak of the South African (Anglo-Boer) War the following year diverted European attention from these turbulent matters. The Swazi profited from both sides as spies and runners—and by absconding with Transvaal cattle sent for safekeeping into Swaziland—but no Swazi regiments actually saw action. King Bunu died, broken and dissolute, during the war. The council's choice of his infant son Sobhuza II (d. 1982) as successor was based largely on the perceived need to reassert Dlamini legitimacy following such a stormy and unpopular reign. Sobhuza's mother, Lomawa Ndwandwe (d. 1938), was the ideal candidate for queen mother, being directly descended from the royal line of Zwide. The deceased Bunu's mother, Gwamile, and his brother, Malunge (d. 1915), acted as regents. Their courage and resoluteness were to be both needed and severely tested during the trying years that lay ahead.

Upon the war's conclusion in 1902, Britain assumed the role of protector over Swaziland. The country was administered first through a special commissioner, who was responsible (to the British governor of the Transvaal) for policing the territory, collecting tax, and implementing the laws of the Transvaal, which were applied to Swaziland virtually unchanged. Only a skeletal administrative staff was provided. Given that, and their previous bitter experience in attempting to disarm the Basotho (which had touched off a war the Basotho had won), the British authorities were worried about enforcing a similar disarmament decree in Swaziland. But in the event, the Swazi proved entirely tractable in giving up the arms they had acquired during the war. Zulu police were used in the collection of the tax. These and other measures dashed initial Swazi hopes that British victory in the war would result in the restoration of Swazi sovereignty and the expulsion of the concessionaires.

The Swazi could scarcely have known that even as they entertained those visions of their deliverance by the British, they were being swept up in the transformation of the political economy of the entire subcontinent, effected largely by the needs of British capital in South Africa. The transition from open to underground mining in the diamond fields in the 1880s, combined with the discovery of gold on the Witwatersrand in the same

Sobhuza II with his grandmother, Queen Regent Labotsibene (Gwamile), 1903. Photo from the Swaziland National Archives.

decade, created a massive new demand for reliable supplies of low-cost and disciplined labor that existing sources—regional African subsistence farming economies—gave no hope of supplying. It was a demand that was multiplied by the labor requirements of other enterprises developing in support of mining: roads, railroads, and harbors; the construction of buildings, indeed, entire towns; manufacturing, processing, and service industries; and others. Most notably, agricultural production to supply the food requirements of the new industrial labor force created a competing demand for farm labor.

Researchers have begun to discover the ways in which the resulting "ruthless and insatiable" call for labor transformed the preindustrial economies of southern Africa in the late nineteenth and early twentieth centuries. Some have argued that the European wars conducted against them in the 1870s and 1880s (the attacks on the Zulu and the Basotho, for instance) were essentially the violent preconditions to the later process of proletarianization.[21] In even more instances, subtler forms of coercion, such as taxation and land reservation, aimed at plucking farmers from their lands and placing them in the migrant labor stream, were seen at work. The crucial factor that so decisively distinguished the South Africa of the 1870s from that of the turn of the century was the willingness (some would say enthusiasm) of the latter state to intervene in this process of proletarianization. Critically for Swaziland, the demands of capital in South Africa meant that the process came to be carried out in areas kept separate politically from South Africa, but that remained for all practical purposes well within what came to be known as its labor "catchment area." "It was only with the enormously important intervention of the state," two leading proponents of this theory argue, "first in the form of taxation and later in land reservation, together with its increasing ability to intervene in labour markets beyond South Africa's political boundaries, that supplies began to meet demand."[22] The British high commissioner for South Africa, Sir Alfred Milner, held a decidedly Victorian ideal of the new regional political economy even before the war. In 1897 he talked of the entire subcontinent as far north as the Zambezi as a European preserve based on a tightly controlled African labor force.[23] That was the context in which the events in Swaziland between the Boer War and World War I, which resulted in a major upheaval of existing property relations and the beginnings of Swazi proletarianization, must be viewed. Indeed, it was Milner himself, in his capacity as governor of the Transvaal, who oversaw those events.

Milner remained in this capacity from the conclusion of the Boer War until 1905, when he was succeeded by Lord Selborne. Selborne continued to administer Swaziland until the Transvaal itself became self-governing in 1907, when administration of the kingdom was transferred to the British high commissioner—largely a technicality, since Selborne had been both governor and high commissioner until that time. But now a resident commissioner was stationed at Mbabane, with a full administrative staff. Swaziland, which was never officially proclaimed a British protectorate, was until 1968 administered exactly like those other states in southern Africa that had been so declared by the Colonial Office through the high commissioner for South Africa—Basutoland and the Bechuanaland Protectorate.

Under these arrangements, the traditional structure of Swazi governance, the district chiefs and the queen regent and council at Lobamba, were kept in place but were made conspicuously subordinate to the British administration. The "native" court system thus remained, but now with appellate authority falling to the resident commissioner, who also held primary jurisdiction over capital crimes. The queen regent and chiefs were placed on salary, and the British forbade use of the title "king" in reference to the youthful Sobhuza. Until 1967, virtually the eve of independence, he was the "paramount chief."

The essential problem to be dealt with by the new colonial government was the land, and it is on that issue that the effects of state intervention on behalf of British capital can most clearly be seen. Concession documents, validated by the 1890 court enquiry, had placed Swaziland (albeit in a confused fashion) entirely in foreign hands. The Swazi maintained that Mbandzeni had not ceded the land, only leased it, and that in any event a king had no constitutional right to alienate land.

But in fact, with the establishment of British protection, the land issue had gone beyond the Swazi question of legitimacy. The permanent settler population was nearing 1,000, and its overriding concern was the capital development of Swaziland. Two preconditions were essential. There had to be unquestioned freehold tenure of the concessioned land. There also had to be created an abundant and reliable source of cheap labor. Events proved that the settlers, not the Swazi monarchy, held the ear of the high commissioner.

The upshot was that despite heated Swazi opposition, a concessions commission was empowered in 1904 to delineate boundaries and to establish the priority of claims. In 1907 its findings were promulgated in the high commissioner's Partition Proclamation.[24] That document represented a resounding victory for the settlers. One-third of the land was reserved for the Swazi, the bulk of the remainder being awarded to the whites in secure and unfettered tenure.[25] Territory that was neither designated as "Native Area" or assigned to a concessionaire was to be held in reserve as Crown Land, available for future grant or lease by the high commissioner. Minerals were held separate from this arrangement, the rights to be awarded separately by the colonial state. Thus, minerals known or discovered to be on Native Area land belonged to the colonial state and were open (with its permission) to European prospecting and development.

Once the demarcation was completed, Swazi were allowed a five-year grace period before actually being forced from their former lands. Actual demarcation was carried out by a single commissioner, George Grey, in 1908, by which action thirty-two Native Areas were designated variously throughout Swaziland. Those boundaries were legitimized by the high commissioner in 1909, meaning that by 1 July 1914 Swazi heads of household had either to make tenancy arrangements with their new European landlords or remove themselves to a Native Area.

For dependency theorists, Swaziland during this period can be seen as a classic example of deliberate underdevelopment by the colonial state, with the dual intent of expropriating the means of production and creating a labor force. The key to the process of underdevelopment was the small but effectively organized and determined cadre of white concessionaires, mainly English-speaking and backed by British capital, who seized upon the opportunity of a new and sympathetic British presence to legitimize concessions of highly questionable origin and propriety.[26] The leader of the cabal was Allister Miller (d. 1951), who as manager of the Swaziland Corporation, publisher of the *Times of Swaziland*, head of the Swaziland Farmers' Association, political gadfly, and entrepreneur of Rhodes's stamp, enjoyed a commanding sway in the affairs of Swaziland for the next half century.[27]

Miller habitually talked of the "denationalization" and the "detribalization" of the Swazi as goals. "It is my opinion," he wrote to the high commissioner in 1906, "that [the Swazi] must be freed . . . certainly and consistently, from the exclusiveness of tribal life." The aim of any partition scheme, in other words, was to so restrict the Native Area that the Swazi would have insufficient land to provide for population growth beyond half a generation, "in the interests of [European] land development by local cheap and plentiful labour."[28]

That was what happened. The partition awarded the Swazi 2,420 out of a total area of 6,553 square miles (3,872 out of 10,485 sq km) for their thirty-two Native Areas. Given Miller's reckoning that "native communes are doubling their population every 25 years," that left thirteen years of land sufficiency to accommodate demographic growth—fewer for cattle increase—before significant overcrowding began.[29] Even those calculations were made on the assumption that a significant proportion of Swazi homesteaders would cut deals with their new landlords and remain as tenant farmer/laborers rather than move to the reserves. That, too, was government policy. "I want many of the Swazi," the high commissioner wrote in 1908, "to stay on the farmers' land and work for them the way they do in the Transvaal."[30] Multitudes of Swazi did stay, 15,000-odd of them, typically agreeing to labor for six months of the year for ten shillings per month for the right to remain on the land in return. Some received no wages at all.

The actual delineation of the Native Areas by Commissioner Grey further restricted Swazi productivity by assigning to them the poorest-quality land. Jonathan Crush figures that of the total areas of the reserves, 79 percent was composed of soil types ranging from poor to untillable, and of the remainder, nearly a third was on slopes greater than fourteen degrees. That left 15 percent of the reserves with soils and slopes well suited to crop production. Of the settler area, by contrast, nearly 70 percent

22

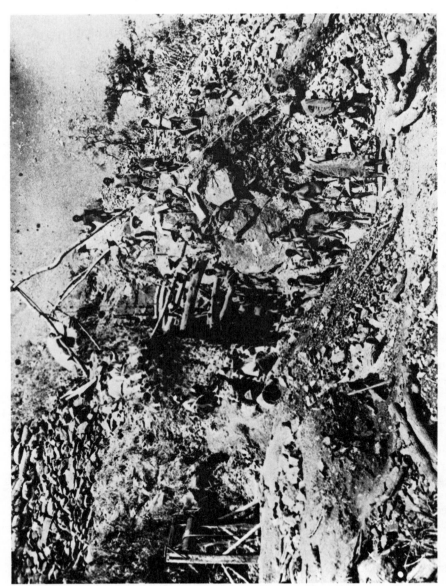

Gold mine, Komati River, 1888. On the left is a prospect shaft. Photo from the Swaziland National Archives.

was ideal for crops.[31] All of the known minerals fell into the settler area, as well as all the water needed to mine and process them and to irrigate crops to feed the required labor.

Removal of the Swazi to the reserves was carried out during 1914. Native Areas in the south (Hlatikulu District) and west (Mankaiana District) were particularly rocky, hilly, and barren. By 1932, the year of Sir Alan Pim's *Report on the Economic Condition of Swaziland*, those areas especially were becoming "overpopulated" and "seriously overstocked."[32] By the early 1940s conditions there had become so poor[33] that a chagrined British government embarked upon a scheme of subsidized land purchase and settlement in order to check further deterioration of the population/land ratio.

The queen regent, Gwamile, proved powerless to prevent these events. Her pleadings and remonstrances culminated in the dispatch of a deputation of five chiefs to London in 1907 to protest what was being done.[34] It was to no avail. Faced at every turn with a firm colonial determination to proceed with the expropriation, Gwamile ultimately sought recourse in the young men of her nation. In 1907 she urged them to seek work in the gold mines of South Africa and to contribute a quarter of their earnings, £5 per year, to a fund to buy back the land.[35]

State exaction of surplus through high taxation,[36] combined with periodic Swazi levies to finance protest deputations, repurchase land, and educate the young king, made the Swazi the most heavily taxed population in southern Africa. Consequently, after the expulsion of 1914, the Swazi progressively became a nation of migrant laborers. Shifting agriculturalists were first immobilized through the delineation of the reserves, then semiproletarianized by the need to round out subsistence needs and to pay tax. A nation that had been self-supporting until the cattle epidemics of the 1890s now became a chronic importer of grains. Swaziland's dependency on imported foodstuffs continues to this day.

THE EVOLUTION OF A PROTECTORATE (1914–1945)

The "denationalization" of the Swazi in this manner thereafter shaped virtually every aspect—political, economic, and social—of society after 1914. Swaziland between the wars became a virtual model of Milner's grand design, a self-governing white community supported by a black labor force; British colonial policy made it so.

That policy was based on the assumption that Swaziland would eventually be incorporated into white-ruled South Africa. The kingdom had been excluded from the Union in 1909 (along with Basutoland and the Bechuanaland Protectorate) in a British fit of "trusteeship conscience" during the Liberal government years, but that exclusion was meant to be only temporary.[37] The territories would be incorporated once Parliament was assured that the rights of the Africans were preserved (in accordance with a schedule attached to the Union constitution itself), and it was assumed that Swaziland would be the first to be so handled, perhaps in as little as ten years. As it happened, incorporation never took place, largely because of London's reaction to the treatment of Africans in South Africa. But the assumption that the British were in Swaziland as "temporary tenants" (in the Colonial Office's words) underlay the shaping of all colonial policy there.[38] Milner himself, as colonial secretary (1919–1921), gave that strategy the imprimatur of that office when he spoke of Swaziland as the least favorable territory for self-government, being the most likely candidate of the "Scheduled Territories" for transfer. "White settlement is important and is bound to grow," he wrote, "and [the] country is inseparable economically from adjoining districts of [the] Transvaal."[39]

The colonial administration did much during the years around World War I to hasten the fulfillment of its own predictions. Various subsidized white-settlement schemes were implemented, notably the Mushroom Land Settlement Company in 1909 (the brainstorm of Allister Miller) and the postwar Returned Soldiers Settlement Scheme. The European population doubled between 1911 and 1921, to 2,200. The imperial ambitions of both Milner and Miller were behind each scheme: to strengthen the country's white population with English-speakers in particular, to counterbalance the preponderence of Afrikaner farmers, especially in the lowveld.[40] Neither scheme achieved the successes envisioned, either in attracting great numbers or in diluting the Boers in the south. More often that not, returned soldier "settlers" who purchased freehold tracts for a few shillings per acre turned out to be speculators who sold out at the first opportunity, many times to Afrikaners.

Those who did settle in Swaziland, Briton or Afrikaner, grew maize where rainfall permitted and in the lowlands grazed cattle (Allister Miller and the Swaziland Corporation established the Bar-R Ranch in the lowveld near Big Bend). By the 1920s many were branching into tobacco and cotton, both labor-intensive cash crops. Many Swazi who remained on European-owned land after 1914 as tenants became cash-crop and ranching laborers. At the same time, gold and tin mining gradually became uneconomic and died out, sending early entrepreneurs like David Forbes into farming and ranching. It would not be until the discovery of asbestos in the north and the establishment of the mine at Havelock in 1938 that the mining industry would again become a significant employer. Swazi migrant labor abroad, to South Africa's mines and farms, continued apace during those years.

European prosperity in the teens and twenties failed to match even the modest growth of the white population. Crops failed from lack of water; farms failed for want of good management; even the Bar-R Ranch went under. But the whites (mainly British) made use of the labor and the knowledge of their Swazi tenants, and their lot gradually improved. Certainly their political influence did. In response to settler pressure the European Advisory Council was established in 1921, and throughout the colonial years it and its successor bodies became increasingly formal and effective lobbying influences on colonial administrations in behalf of settler

Weighing cotton in the lowveld, 1920s. Photo from the Swaziland National Archives.

European Advisory Council, 1921. Allister Miller is seated second from left; third from left is de Symon Honey, resident commissioner of Swaziland (1917–1928). Photo from the Swaziland National Archives.

interests. So too did farmers' organizations *cum* pressure groups: the Siteki, the Southern, and the Swaziland farmers' associations. Each became dominated by English-speaking settlers and, consequently, increasingly opposed (beginning in the 1920s) to Swaziland's incorporation into the Union, barring one consideration. Many saw the building of a railroad as the key to access to South Africa's markets for their cattle and crops at competitive prices, and many—perhaps most—would have agreed to transfer in return for that. (If Afrikaner blood sentiment centering in the south had had its way, Swaziland would have joined the Union on any account.)

That the fostering and subsidizing of those developments was the result of official British policy was best evidenced during the colonial secretaryship of L. S. Amery (1924–1929). Amery toured southern Africa in 1927, when he met with the European Advisory Council and the various farmers' organizations in Swaziland. He came away with the strong impression that the key to the policy of timely transfer was to make Swaziland "effectively British before it goes into the Union"; that to attempt it "before a prosperous and contented British community was established there" would be undesirable.[41]

Amery therefore entered into a commitment to the Swaziland settlers on the spot, which resulted in loan guarantees of up to £128,500 for credit to settlers, capital development, and administration. Various British settlement schemes were initiated or revived. And it was during this period that the South African Railway Board introduced bus and bulk hauling service into Swaziland, connecting the main settlement and agricultural areas to the railheads at Breyten, Golela, and Piet Retief. That, in turn, led to the upgrading of the road system connecting the settler-dominated areas.[42]

That the British settler community before World War II developed neither the numbers nor the prosperity that Amery had envisioned was due to circumstances beyond his control. South African agricultural subsidies, cattle import restrictions (beginning in 1924), and marketing boards effectively kept Swaziland from competing fairly in South African markets. The 1930s depression hit Swaziland as hard as any region in southern Africa: It hindered development of communications and helped restrict settler immigration. Much freehold land remained absentee-owned and undeveloped, in fact, well beyond the war.

As for the Swazi themselves, British policy in the interwar years (centering as it did upon the assumption of transfer) was one of studied neglect. It was "studied" insofar as Swaziland was designed to serve British capital (both South African mining and local settler) as a labor reserve, which had been an original aim of colonial taxation and land policies. Consequently, aside from a few cosmetic projects for Swazi (duly given play in the annual reports), capital resources favored settler development in the form of roads and communications, irrigation schemes, agricultural loans, and so forth. Since the better part of those funds came from the "native tax," such development was in effect subsidized by the Swazi.

Meanwhile, as both human and stock population increased in the Native Areas, so too did conditions there deteriorate and, as Lord Milner and Allister Miller had envisioned, Swazi options for survival narrowed to one: migrant labor. By 1920 upwards of 25 percent—probably closer to 40 percent, there is no telling the exact numbers—of the male working population (age eighteen to forty-five) was absent in the Transvaal at any given time.[43] Their recruitment was organized by the Native Recruiting Corporation (NRC, the recruiting arm of the Transvaal Chamber of Mines in Swaziland), which had begun its Swaziland operations in 1913. By the mid-1920s local migration from the Native Areas to settler ranches and cotton and tobacco fields was also becoming a significant supplement to the tenant labor already residing on European land. How the prolonged removal of this vital element drained homestead productivity and affected social relations of all kinds has yet to be measured, but the effects are likely to be on the scale found among the neighboring Zulu.[44] They were bad enough for one colonial official to refer to Swaziland by the early 1930s as "the least reputable and most neglected of the British dependencies."[45]

The colonial administration characteristically placed the blame for reduced agricultural output on Swazi backwardness in cultivation and herd management. A few African agricultural demonstrators were trained and stationed in the field, and some attempts were made to generate Swazi export crop production. But the efforts were minimal, and the effects even less. Amery on his 1927 tour was shocked by what he saw. "What I felt most," he wrote later, "was that we had done so little for the Protectorates ourselves; that instead of . . . raising the general standard of their peoples, we had been content to protect them from outside interference [sic], leaving them to carry on under a very unproductive form of indirect tribal rule as museum pieces, human Whipsnades, in an Africa that was being transformed at a breathless pace." Yet Amery's answer was, once more, to "build up a prosperous British community" while developing the Africans in "education, etc., . . . till they were more fit to stand up to the impact of transfer."[46] That was what in essence happened, and government efforts in that area were still minimal. The administration, in the year of Amery's visit, was running one government school for the Swazi and helping to maintain another eleven mission schools with an annual grant of £1,350. Health care was also in the hands of the missions.[47]

There was much more to Swazi politics during the years to 1945 than Amery's offhand comment about "unproductive . . . indirect tribal rule" would indicate. It was true, as the colonial secretary argued, that the British aim had been to maintain the hold of the monarchy over the people in a truncated form, while reducing its leverage with the resident commissioner to the level of symbolism. In this it was largely successful. The state made itself supreme in all important judicial matters. It reduced the monarchy's private (concession) revenue from £12,000 to £1,000 per year while placing the queen regent, Gwamile, and the principal chiefs on government salary in return for their assistance in maintaining order and collecting the tax.

In response to these pressures, Gwamile during her regency (1899–1921) was forced to play simultaneously two supremely delicate and intricate roles. The first was to protect her people and their lands as best she could, and in that she failed: The Swazi were, after all, removed from two-thirds of their lands and partly proletarianized. Only her force of character enabled her to achieve the very modest gains she made.

Her second task was to restore the legitimacy of the monarchy in the face of a disillusioned citizenry and an inimical colonial administration. In that, she had her work cut out for her. Two prodigal and dissolute kings at the end of the nineteenth century (Mbandzeni and Bunu) had left the Swazi royal house in disarray, its authority and even its legitimacy questioned widely among its subjects. In the restoration of Dlamini legitimacy Gwamile was remarkably successful. One way she accomplished this was to prepare young Sobhuza for the tasks that awaited him as king. Gwamile had once opposed the education of her own son, Bunu, and had lived to regret that after he became king. Now the colonial threat was even more complex. "In what does the white man's power lie?" she asked. "It lies in money and in books. We too will learn; we too will be rich."[48] Gwamile established a special school at Zombodze for Sobhuza and companion princes and notables, and in 1916 she sent him off to Lovedale College in the Cape. The future king returned to Swaziland before completing his degree there, but the dividends that Gwamile's foresight paid toward the character of his future reign were incalculable.

Gwamile's efforts in a second direction were more mixed in their results. "We too will be rich," she had said. One of the keys to the revival of the monarchy lay in securing a substantial and unassailable economic base for it. Her initial efforts were more fruitful in increasing her stature among her people for standing up to the British than in improving her financial position. The issue in the early 1900s was the continuance of the Private Revenue Concession, which had paid the monarchy £12,000 annually, and which had been in the possession of the Transvaal government since the early 1890s. During the Anglo-Boer War, revenue accumulating in the fund had been held in escrow in Pretoria, so that by the time the British came to control it, it amounted to some £45,000. The British, whose aim was to maintain Swazi royal dependency, stymied Gwamile's every attempt to obtain both accumulated principal and income, using all the arbitrary actions and deception required.

In 1903 Gwamile requested an accounting and asked that the fund be transferred to her, along with the renewal of the £12,000 annual income. This Lord Milner, the British high commissioner, refused. There was only £20,000 in the escrow account, he informed her. It was to be established as the Private Revenue Trust, whose purpose would be to facilitate projects of benefit to all Swazi, such as dipping tanks to eradicate tick-borne cattle disease. Then, on the grounds that £12,000 was an excessive annual sum,

Milner cut back her income to £1,000 per year (to be paid from the Private Revenue Trust), adding an annual allowance of £800 from the colonial administration. Secretly, Milner then used the remaining escrow balance of £25,000 to purchase from certain concessionaires the customs, transport, and other concessions essential to governing the country.[49]

In such manner were colonial dependencies created. Gwamile remonstrated at what was being done. She receipted her first trust fund payment with a protest: She was owed £85,000, not £20,000.[50] She charged the 1907 land deputation to look into the matter of the Private Revenue Concession with London. Her efforts availed nothing.

Gwamile then turned to other means to capitalize the independence of the royal house. Some of her designs were open, some not, but all centered on the royal power to tax. She dispatched labour migrants to Johannesburg, with one-quarter of their wages to go into a land repurchase fund. Both she and Prince Malunge recruited their subjects for migrant labor in return for capitation fees. Royal levies established the "Swazi National Fund" to pay for the young king's education and to eradicate cattle disease. Funds were exacted to pay for the 1907 and 1923 deputations to Britain; to purchase aircraft for the Royal Air Force during World War I; to support the African National Congress in Johannesburg; for any number of purposes. All levies were collectible in cash or in cattle, and special delegations were dispatched to collect from workers in the Rand gold mines.

How much money thus found its way to Zombodze no one knew, least of all the exasperated colonial administration. But if the mounting reaction of the people being taxed was any indication, it was considerable. As levy followed levy, the mood of acquiescence changed to suspicion and on occasion to outright opposition. It came to be widely believed that a great deal of the money collected stuck to the palms of the collectors and that much of the remainder was used by the royal house for other than the announced purposes. At times a suspicious colonial administration moved to straighten out affairs, but it never got to see the account books at Zombodze. Gradually, the reluctance of the citizenry to pay more grew, and in some cases people took to hiding in the hills when the royal collectors were about.[51]

Still, there was no question that it was a renewed and enriched monarchy which the queen regent passed on to Sobhuza II at the time of his investiture as *ngwenyama* in 1921. The great question that loomed at the time of his accession was the "the land," the universal sense of betrayal by the British in its expropriation and the expectation that now that Sobhuza was king he would set things right. Indeed, it is fair to say that "the land" and all that it implied—resources, sovereignty, and much more—dominated royal consciousness and maneuverings for the succeeding quarter century, in fact throughout the king's reign.

During the early years of his reign Sobhuza was up against impossible odds, an increasingly entrenched settler interest backed up by a determined

The 1923 land deputation to London. Sobhuza II is seated, center; seated on the far right is Pixley Ka Izaka Seme. Photo from the Swaziland National Archives.

colonial administration, and his early attempts at redress were inauspicious. He headed a deputation to London in 1923, which was rebuffed. In 1924 he engaged his barrister and adviser, Dr. Pixley Ka Izaka Seme,[52] in a lawsuit before the Special Court of Swaziland to reverse the ejection of some of his subjects from lands covered by the Unallotted Lands Concession. The case was lodged officially against Allister Miller, from whose farm the expulsion had occurred, but it was in fact a test case of the validity of all the concessions. The court dismissed the suit, and a subsequent appeal to the Privy Council in London was denied in 1926.

Frustrated by a law system he could not control, the king turned during the following decade to practicing some European guile on the Europeans themselves. Several times, notably in 1937 and 1938, the *ngwenyama* hinted at his willingness to negotiate on the question of transfer to the Union in return for a land settlement favorable to the Swazi. He had been adamant against such action as a newly crowned king; opposition to it had been a principal reason for the 1923 deputation. But in 1937 he indicated to the British high commissioner his willingness to consider transfer, but "the terms would have to be very good indeed." A year later he again toyed with the issue: "When a young man comes to woo a girl he first places his gifts before her." Sobhuza, the prospective bride, wanted land returned to Swazi control, guarantees for the integrity and status of his nation, and the "preservation of native institutions"—his habitual terminology for the maintenance of royal hegemony.[53] Here the *ngwenyama* was playing the Europeans at their own game, testing diplomatic skills for which he later would become legendary; that neither his people nor his councillors would stand for transfer he knew well.

Nothing came of these moves. By 1941 overpopulation and overstocking in the Native Areas had become so serious that Sobhuza in council petitioned the British king in Parliament for redress. Britain, now in need of colonial support and resources as never before in its war with Germany, responded. In 1940 Colonial Welfare and Development funds went for the repurchase of European-held lands, and the bulk of the remaining Crown Lands (until then reserved for European purchase) were earmarked for Swazi use. In 1946, as part of Britain's empirewide venture into social experimentation in the colonies, a Native Land Settlement Scheme was launched utilizing these new lands, which, with subsequent additions, totaled nearly 350,000 acres (141,750 ha). Its goals, relief of population pressure and the securing of the economic future of the peasantry through managed cultivation and stock raising on redistributed lands, fell short of achievement. But the Swazi thereby regained much land. In 1944 the drive toward reclaiming the land was supplemented by Sobhuza's inauguration of the Lifa Fund, a levy on Swazi cattle and cash for the repurchase of more territory. By independence in 1968, 56 percent of the land lay in Swazi hands.

CAPITAL PENETRATION AND ITS CONSEQUENCES (1945–1963)

World War II marked a major turning point in the economic history of Swaziland. In the years that followed it, the kingdom became the theater of massive penetration and development by foreign capital. Those events occurred on settler holdings and specially earmarked Crown Lands, not on Swazi-held territory. In 1947 a South African consortium backed by British capital established in northern Swaziland the beginnings of what is now the second largest commercial forestry complex (by acreage) in the world. The Anglo-American Corporation, which has acquired a growing interest in this timber and pulp venture, has also extracted iron ore and operates the largest coal mine in the country. In 1950 the Colonial (now Commonwealth) Development Corporation (CDC) capitalized an extensive network of irrigation projects in the middleveld and lowveld that produced a major citrus fruit and sugar industry within a decade.[54] Sugar was to become Swaziland's largest source of foreign exchange; but light manufacturing and food processing, centered in the Matsapha and Nhlangano industrial sites, along with tourism, further diversified capital investment.[55]

The magnitude of the development and construction involved (Peak Timbers Ltd. by the early 1950s had planted 60,000 acres [24,000 ha] of trees and constructed 750 miles [1,200 km] of roads) created an unprecedented demand for local labor. Recruiters traveled the countryside with buses, offering even better wages and improved working conditions as the years went by and the labor market tightened. South African gold and coal mine recruiters were hard put to make their labor quotas, and some of them withdrew. The pressure of increasing numbers of people and cattle in the Native Areas seemingly became less acute, given the readily available employment opportunities for men, women, and children. Those were the years of heavy local employment of foreign labor, from Mozambique, the Transvaal, even Nyasaland.

By 1962, however, the labor shortage had turned into a surplus. Mechanization in agriculture, a leveling off of construction and cropping locally and of gold mine employment on the Witwatersrand, a jump in the numbers of school leavers, all combined with a demographic growth rate that was nearly doubling the population every generation, had created an oversupply of labor. Local industries responded by effectively freezing wages and reducing other incentives, whereupon laborers in every key industry organized themselves into increasingly militant unions. Part of the problem lay in the widespread worker perception that the established grievance procedure, based on a system of king's representatives (*tindvuna*) at every work site, was ineffective. That sentiment, in turn, provided fertile ground for the activism of politically ambitious men with an eye toward the approach of independence. The result was a wave of strikes during 1962 and 1963, beginning in timber and spreading with increasing unruliness to the asbestos and sugar industries. By June 1963 neither the colonial administration nor the king was sure of the power to contain events. A state of emergency was declared, and a British army battalion was flown in from Kenya. It remained for five years, and union activity was thenceforward progressively reduced in substance, if not in appearance.

These new economic realities were one of the major postwar changes that profoundly affected Swazi domestic politics. The massive infusion of foreign capital into Swaziland created powerful new extraterritorial interests (initially British) that combined with settler organizations traditionally opposed to incorporation into the Union. In later years, as South African investment came to predominate in Swaziland, and the rest of black Africa hardened its position against trade with South Africa, the logic of using the kingdom as an "independent" exporter of South African capitalized goods and produce made the maintenance of Swaziland's separateness increasingly attractive to South African interests as well.

The second factor affecting local politics was the reversal of the British intention to transfer Swaziland to the Union following the Nationalist victory in the 1948 South African election. Actually, the hardening of the British position had occurred well before 1948. Official statements to that effect were being made before the end of the war, and by 1946 the Dominions Office was referring to the prospect as "nothing but a Nationalist pipe-dream."[56] Consequently, the colonial administration from 1944 onward began issuing a series of proclamations aimed at enhancing the power of the Swazi monarchy to act as its agent in the perpetuation of indirect rule. "Native authorities" proclamations had previously been promulgated in Bechuanaland (1934) and Basutoland (1938), and the intention was to model the 1944 Native Administration Proclamation in Swaziland on them. But the king effectively manipulated the process to secure and improve his own position.

The antecedents of the *ngwenyama's* decisive actions during the 1960s and 1970s to ensure the reproduction of the monarchy are clearly found in his maneuverings before the various "native administration" proclamations of 1944 and 1950. The king in council repeatedly faced down the administration over a series of issues involving respective powers as those proclamations were drafted. The result was that the Swaziland laws (in contradistinction to those of Bechuanaland and Basutoland) effectively removed the colonial state as the initiator and controller of local administration in favor of the king, placing the state more in the position of "on occasion exercis[ing] a veto in certain directions." The Native Courts and the National Treasury Proclamations of 1950 restored the monarchy's criminal jurisdiction, which had been withdrawn in 1904, and its independent authority over a portion of the native tax. The lawmaking and enforcement powers thus conferred on the Swazi royal house placed Swaziland dramatically apart from the other dependencies in its sovereignty over the traditional political economy.[57]

The Swazi monarchy was consequently able to enter into the dealings leading to independence during the 1960s with powers far greater than those possessed by the Basotho or Tswana monarchies. It is important to understand, in conclusion, that the causes for that difference lay in a series of actions initiated throughout the twentieth century, first by Gwamile and subsequently by Sobhuza, aimed at restoring the economic and political sovereignty of the royal house, which had been first squandered by their immediate predecessors and then wrested away by the colonials. It is fair to say that the power over the traditional sector enjoyed by Sobhuza upon approaching independence was in every important way greater than that held by his father upon his death in 1899. That power, in turn, would lead to the securing of royal dominance over the political economy of Swaziland during the 1960s and 1970s, an outcome that had been by no means predestined. Control over the traditional society was especially important because in Swaziland traditional institutions and customs play such powerful roles in the regulation and conduct of daily life. It is to the examination of those institutions that we turn in the following chapter.

2

The Sociocultural System

TRADITIONAL SOCIETY: THE BASIS OF CONSERVATISM AND THE FORCES FOR CHANGE

Swazi society places great emphasis on traditionalism and conservative values, partly in response to the stresses that have confronted it over the past two centuries. In addition, its rulers have consciously (sometimes forcibly) emphasized those ideals as the guiding ideology of the nation, which, remaining predominantly rural, generally accepts them. But as society becomes more highly industrialized and urbanized, and as it achieves better education, many of those values are being questioned and on occasion challenged. Social change has brought stress. This chapter describes the basis of Swazi traditional life and examines how modern values are influencing change.

The social basis of traditional daily life in the countryside during the early 1980s remains much as Hilda Kuper described it in her renowned *An African Aristocracy* over thirty-five years previously. Challenges to those values, which have come with postwar capital development, are seen most readily in the urban areas and in the changing economics and hence sociology of the rural homestead. This chapter relies heavily on Kuper's original study and subsequent analyses to describe that traditional society. More recent studies, which often themselves take their departure from Kuper, detail socioeconomic responses to modern forces.[1]

Rapid postwar industrialization and urbanization have not altered the fact that the principal Swazi social unit remains the homestead. Its structure continues much according to tradition. Men dominate, whether as headmen of large, multi-unit homesteads or as fathers of single (perhaps polygynous) families. Polygyny, still prevalent, is less popular among the young, as women seek greater status and jobs, and as homestead economics stress wage income over farm surpluses as a foundation.

Central to the traditional homestead is the cattle byre, a circular area enclosed by substantial logs interspaced with branches. The cattle byre has great ritual as well as practical significance, stemming from the importance of cattle as a store of wealth and symbol of prestige. Formerly,

34

when women were barred from working with cattle, their access to the cattle byre was severely limited. In former times also, the cattle byre contained the sealed grain pits, large and flask-shaped, so that in time of war the homestead's centralized resources (grain and cattle) were more easily defended. The arrangement also ensured male domination of the food supply; but since it also resulted in high rates of spoilage, modern homesteads (at least the wealthier ones) are likely to have above-ground, metal grain storage tanks.

Facing the cattle byre is the great hut, often occupied by the mother or the first wife of the headman. The importance of the mother, in all homestead affairs as in national politics, is central. She represents the link between the head-of-homestead and his lineage, which gives him standing. The traditional "beehive" hut of dried grass has largely been supplanted by mud brick thatched huts or, more recently, cement block structures with metal roofs. Alongside the main hut, often in a reed enclosure, are separate structures for sleeping, cooking, or storage. In a polygynous homestead, each wife normally has her own huts and yard, surrounded by reed fences for privacy, senior wives being closest to the main hut. In substantial homesteads there will also be structures used as bachelors' quarters and guest accommodations. Beyond are the unfenced gardens, irregular as to shape and placement, and still farther away are the grazing lands.

Often a large homestead will embrace more than a single biological family. Kinsmen of various sorts, divorcees, widows or widowers returned to the family, children of full-time city workers, are likely to be occupants. Often also, heads of homesteads in a particular region are related by blood or marriage.

Regional groupings of homesteads constitute districts, ruled by chiefs, who are placed by and are responsible to the king. Chiefs are most often princes or heads of important clans. Districts, which can encompass 20 square miles (52 sq km) and include several thousand inhabitants, are commonly subdivided into wards, each with an *induna* (official) with authority delegated by the chief.

Recent years have witnessed significant changes in the demographics and the socioeconomic base of the typical rural household. Kuper theorized in 1947 that the size of the average commoner's homestead would decrease as new economic forces prompted youths to seek wage employment in the urban areas, but that has not happened. Recent research indicates a numerical increase of upwards of 35 percent, to an average of ten persons per rural homestead, by 1981. No one is quite sure why.[2] But social scientists have given us a clearer picture of how the economic base of the homestead has changed in recent years and how these changes have affected domestic strategies.

The dominant phenomenon has been the progressive integration of the homestead's economic base into the modern economy, as evidenced by its increasing dependence on wages. Cash income, averaging E 1,915 per homestead, accounted for more than half (56 percent) of total income

Two Swazi homesteads: in the lowveld near Sitobela (*above*) and in the middleveld near Mahlanya (*below*). Photos by the author.

TABLE 2.1

Contributions by Source to Annual Swazi Homestead Income

Source	Mean Income Per Homestead (E)	% Contribution
i) Contributions to Cash Income		
Wage earnings of homestead-based (commuter) workers	544	50.6
Cash remittances from absentee workers	238	22.1
Homestead-based non-agricultural activities	133	12.4
Crop sales (net of crop expenditures)	93	8.7
Livestock sales	67	6.2
Total	1,075	100
ii) Contributions to Income in Kind		
Livestock a) homestead self-consumption	79	9.4
b) increase in livestock weight including births, net of sales, slaughter and deaths	354	42.1
Consumed crop production	137	16.3
In-kind remittances (food, clothing, furniture, agricultural implements/supplies, etc.)	100	11.9
Miscellaneous	170	20.3
Total	840	100
iii) Contributions to Total Income		
Wage earnings of homestead-based (commuter) workers	544	27.4
Cash and in-kind remittances from absentee workers	338	17.0
Livestock sales/consumption and herd growth	500	25.2
Crop sales and consumption	299	15.1
Homestead-based non-agricultural activities	133	6.7
Miscellaneous	170	8.6
Total	1,984	100

Source: Fion de Vletter, "A Socio-Economic Profile of Swazi Rural Homesteads: A Summary of the Main Findings Arising From the Swaziland Rural Homestead Survey" (Kwaluseni: Social Science Research Unit, University of Swaziland, 1982).

in 1982; and of that, almost three-quarters was generated from wage employment. By contrast, barely 6 percent of all homesteads were supporting themselves by crop sales alone. Homesteads earned more cash from non-agricultural activities, such as handicrafts, beer brewing, and traditional medicine, than they did from agricultural sales.[3] Crop and livestock sales each contributed the smallest proportions to cash income, although both crops and livestock, especially an increase in cattle herds, contributed considerably more to *total* (cash plus in-kind) homestead income (see Table 2.1).

TABLE 2.2

Homestead Ownership of Selected Assets

Assets	% Ownership
i) Sample 1150 Homesteads	
Plough	51.2
Crop sprayer	12.2
Car or light truck	13.6
Lorry	.9
Bicycle	27.8
Stove	33.2
Refrigerator	4.3
Beds	85.8
Sofa	16.5
Dressers and/or wardrobes	33.1
Pressing iron	83.4
Sewing machine	32.1
Radio	73.3
Record player	11.0
Tape recorder	13.5
ii) Sample 457 Homesteads	
Planter	20.0
Harrow	17.5
Cultivator	26.0
Wheelbarrow	50.0
Maize grinder	58.0
Maize sheller	3.0
Grain tank	35.0
Scotchcart	5.5
Sledge	31.0
Tractor	1.7
Primus stove	77.2

Source: Fion de Vletter, "A Socio-Economic Profile of Swazi Rural Homesteads: A Summary of the Main Findings Arising From the Swaziland Rural Homestead Survey" (Kwaluseni: Social Science Research Unit, University of Swaziland, 1982).

All cash income—and then some—was expended by the homestead, in the following manner: 40 percent for cropping expenditures and education; 36 percent for food; and 24 percent for "other" expenditures (fuel, clothing, household goods, transportation, and so forth).[4]

A listing of assets from two survey samples (Table 2.2) gives an indication of general rural homestead wealth and viability in 1981. Just over half of the homesteads owned ploughs, but less than one in fifty possessed a tractor; about one in seven owned a car or small truck; nearly one-third were in possession of a sewing machine. About three-quarters had primus stoves and radios. In the aggregate, survey information indicated that by 1981 one in ten households was relatively wealthy, while one in five was "impoverished," resulting in "extreme" homestead differentiation. At the least, it seems fair to assume that homestead response to modern economic forces (principally wage employment and nonagricultural forms of homestead-based commodity production) has resulted in lesser agricultural self-sufficiency and greater disparity in wealth than prevailed in the precapitalist economy.[5] It seems equally reasonable to conclude that the "rural" homestead remains at present a principal locus of domestic life for most Swazis, including professionals, civil servants, traders, and workers in the modern sector of the economy.

Blood, and blood relationships, are very important in Swazi society. Blood relationships extend far beyond the biological family (established by marriage) that is the heart of each homestead. The blood group embraces the classificatory kinship system, coursing through both maternal and paternal groups, the largest extension of which is the patrilineal clan. Each of them is commonly named after its original founder (e.g., Mamba, Fakudze) or with a praise name. The child inherits the clan name of its father; a woman, upon marriage, retains her clan name. "No Swazi can throw away his blood," the Swazi say; no man "refuses his blood"—abandons a kinsman in trouble—without expecting serious consequences. A kinsman is said to sense danger or mishap to another kinsman, even far away, in the blood.[6] Within clans are smaller groups tracing patrilineal lineages back to common ancestors, sometimes for more than ten generations. Clans and lineages are exogamous, except for the ruling Nkosi Dlamini.[7]

Kuper speaks of a rough hierarchy of clans and even of particular lineages. At the apex is the Nkosi Dlamini, in which the lineage of the king is foremost. Then follow clans that have provided queen mothers (e.g., Simelane, Ndwandwe, Nxumalo); then come clans holding hereditary positions as national officials (e.g. Fakudze, Zwane); finally, there are clans distinguished by the influence, loyalty, or skills of particular individuals (e.g., Vilikati, Mdluli).[8] The Mdluli clan was considerably elevated following the death of Mbandzeni, when his widow, Gwamile Mdluli, was selected as queen mother because of her extraordinary political skills and force of character in the face of the European threat and because of her legendary powers as a rainmaker.

As clan and lineage are vital distinguishing characteristics of the Swazi, so too is age. "The authority of age," says Kuper, "characterises all Swazi behaviour."[9] Age delineation is both individual, by stages throughout one's entire life, and social, by regimentation into cohorts, particularly in the case of men. Kuper describes seven separate growth stages for males (Table 2.3) and ten for females (Table 2.4).

The Swazi have great respect for age. Children are taught to honor their elders, for the aged are the repositories of experience and wisdom. It is the old men and women to whom people turn for advice and guidance in times of doubt and difficulty.

TABLE 2.3

Stages of Growth of Males

Age (approx.)	Swazi Name	Activities	Ritual	Outward Signs
3 months	Luswane	Kept in hut.	Stage ends when child is shown the moon. Receives name.	Wears only protective medicines
In third year	Ummtfwana or Ingane	Carried in a sling. Taught to walk and talk.	Weaned.	Wears nothing or string of beads.
3-8 years	Umfana	Plays a great deal. Herds goats. Plays house.	Kusika tindlebe -- ears cut.	Wears tiny lidjoba -- loin skin.
8-17 years	Lijele	Herds cattle. Responsible messenger.	Puberty ceremony.	Wears loin skin and begins to wear penis cap.
17-27 years	Lijaha or Libungu	Seeks lovers. Enters age class as lijaha. Fighter, hunter. Carefree.	Acceptance of lovers.	Takes pride in appearance. Wears bead ornaments made by lovers.
27-60 years	Indvodza	Married man. Attends councils. Has many responsibilities.	Putting on of head-ring.	Head-ring.
Over 60	Lichegu or Umhlaba	Grandfather. Works less.	Supervises ritual of his sons. Receives great respect.	Head-ring.

Source: Hilda Kuper, An African Aristocracy: Rank Among the Swazi (London: Oxford University Press, 1947).

TABLE 2.4

Stages of Growth of Females

Age (approx.)	Swazi Name	Activities	Ritual	Outward Signs
3 months	Luswane	Kept in hut.	Stage ends when child is shown the moon. Receives name.	Wears only protective medicines.
In third year	Umntfwana or Ingane	Carried in a sling. Taught to walk and talk.	Weaned - bitter aloe rubbed on mother's breast	Wears nothing or string of beads.
6-8 years	Sidzanzane	Plays a good deal. Helps mother, smears floor, learns to grind, plays house (emandlwane).	Ukusika tindlebe -- ears cut.	String of beads and sometimes little skirt of grass or cloth.
8-15 years	Litshitshana	Nurse-maid. Helps in home and in fields.	Ends with puberty ritual.	Skirt of grass or skirt and short toga of cloth. Hair in many styles. Never long. Decorations - bead necklaces.
15-17 years	Lichikiza	Has a lover. Visits his home. Knows a woman's job.	Public selection of sin-gani (lover) in his barracks.	Dresses carefully in mahiya (cloth).
17-22 years	Ingcugce	Ready for marriage. Last fling.	Putting up of hair into high bun. Ends with marriage ceremony.	Though hair is up, bun is still small. Wears dress of cloth.
21-24 years	Makoti or Umlobokati	Bride at husband's home. Works for mother-in-law.	Ritually given permission to behave as wife.	Wears skin apron and skin skirt. Apron worn under armpits (ukwencaya).
24-55 years	Umfati	Wife and mother, tied to home.	Given increasing participation in family ritual.	After birth of 1st child, raises apron over shoulder.
55-65 years	Isalukati	Grandmother. Less work in home: helped by daughters-in-law and grandchildren.	Aids married sons in family ritual.	Less careful of personal appearance.
65 upwards	Umhlaba (earth) or Lidloti (ancestral spirit)	Can do no active work.	Treated with respect due an ancestral spirit.	Usually wears any old clothing.

Source: Hilda Kuper, An African Aristocracy: Rank Among the Swazi (London: Oxford University Press, 1947).

Swazi maidens outside the Lobamba Royal Kraal at the start of the *Umhlanga*, the annual reed dance, in 1965. Photo from the Swaziland National Archives.

In addition, age cohorts constitute an important means of differentiation, among males in particular, and fulfill other important social functions. Cutting across clan lines, they join young men nationwide, at roughly the age of puberty, into a single regiment. Formed every five to seven years by the king, regiments in former times functioned primarily as elements of the national army. Nowadays age cohorts take on important roles in national ritual, serve as labor battalions for the king and nobility throughout the country, and are a principal vehicle for the reproduction and imparting of traditional values. Each cohort has its own name, insignia, songs, officials, and recognized locality (originally military barracks). Impressive evidence of the reverence with which men hold to this system can be seen at any harvest season, when regiments in traditional dress and repeating praise songs, wend their way—often on foot over great distances—to work the king's fields. During World War II Sobhuza called men up by regiments, and nearly 4,000 strong, the Swazi went off to war with the African Pioneer Corps, serving with distinction and on occasion (e.g., at Anzio) conspicuous bravery.

Swazi women also form age classes, but on a distinctly less formal and regimented level. Associations are most often for specific purposes or tasks, tribute labor or ritual (particularly *Umhlanga*) and do not last beyond the event. The *Umhlanga* (Reed Dance) ceremony, although not as ancient or consecrated as the *Incwala*, is nevertheless an important celebration in honor of the queen mother (*ndlovukazi*) and of feminine beauty and virtue. Each July or August, unmarried girls nationwide gather to collect reeds to repair windbreaks around the queen mother's residence. This task is followed by a mass dance in which the girls, dressed only in brief beaded aprons and adornments, show off their beauty and grace to the king and queen mother and to all who come to see. It is a festive and joyous annual reminder of national reverence for the *ndlovukazi* and, by extension, of the importance of women.

The *Umhlanga* ceremony is in a sense exemplary of an aspect of Swazi traditionalism that is increasingly being questioned by the young and the educated. The ceremony venerates the queen mother, but it does not acknowledge or renew her extraordinary powers, as the *Incwala* does the king's. For the young women it celebrates nubility, and in so doing emphasizes the traditional role reserved for Swazi women: procreation and domesticity. Yet as more women become educated and subject to modern influences, fewer remain satisfied with this role alone. In seeking careers and the independence that goes with them, increasing numbers of married women have learned that for them, traditionalism has meant laws which discriminate against them with respect to their tax and legal status as individuals.[10]

Many young women are also reluctant to participate fully any longer in the practice and spirit of the traditional marriage institution. For many, a polygynous marriage is degrading and unacceptable. In fact, in a modernizing society the economics of the institution are restricting it to a smaller circle of affluent men. Similarly, the customs of the levirate (the giving of a widow in marriage to her deceased husband's brother) and the sororate (the giving of a younger sister in place of a deceased wife) are objected to as dehumanizing.

Others question the system of *lobola*, which, to some, smacks of the commoditization of females. *Lobola*, the passage of cattle from the family of the husband to the family of the bride upon marriage, is not, traditionalists argue, simply "the buying and selling of women." It is a symbol, they say, of a woman's past status (women of higher rank command more cattle) and her future security. It is compensation to her family for the loss of her presence and her services, and it ensures the legitimacy of her children and their rights to the benefits of their father's lineage. It further ensures her good treatment at her husband's hands, since his gross mistreatment is grounds for return of the *lobola* cattle if she leaves him. But there is no question that urbanization and education have tempered the practice among certain segments of Swazi society, most often substituting cash for the transfer of cattle, for instance.

The status of women, as reflected in the custom of *lobola* and the *Umhlanga* ceremony is but one aspect of Swazi life in which traditionalism is coming under greater challenge. But as in other areas, change will be too modest and come too slowly to suit some modern sensibilities, for the forces of conservatism and traditionalism in Swaziland are very strong.

Swazi women fashioning a hairdo, a common sight on a Sunday afternoon. Sculptured hair arrangements amount to an art form among Swazi women. Photo by the author.

THE CONSERVATIVE POLITICAL HIERARCHY: THE *NGWENYAMA* AND THE *NDLOVUKAZI*

By tradition Swaziland is a dual monarchy. The king (*ngwenyama*, "the lion") and the queen mother (*ndlovukazi*, "the cow-elephant") together embody all power—legislative, executive, administrative, and religious. Practically speaking, their power was never absolute, for the national council, with its membership of venerable figures, provided guidance and at times exerted strong influence. Since independence the Parliament has often served to moderate authoritarian action. Chiefs have an eye on maintaining the kingship as much as remaining loyal to a particular king, and systems of local government take on initiatives.

Still, there is no dispute as to where the ultimate power lies. The dyarchy by tradition contained its own checks, with the *ngwenyama* and the *ndlovukazi* each reserving certain exclusive powers, each also able to balance certain prerogatives of the other. For instance, the king, who holds most executive and ritual powers, owes his power to the queen mother, whose rank and status, rather than his own qualifications, determine his selection. Their residences are separate as to locality and ritual function; hers is normally regarded as the capital. The king presides over the highest traditional court, but she is in charge of the second highest tribunal, and her homestead provides a sanctuary for those appealing for protection. The king distributes the land, but both he and the queen mother share the powers of rainmaking necessary for its fertility. She has custody of certain sacred national objects, but only his cooperation renders them effective. He has custody and disposition of the royal herds, but she may publicly rebuke him for misusing national wealth. The king is revitalized in the annual *Incwala* ceremony, which takes place at her home. Beyond these formal checks, the queen mother is expected to provide counsel, and if need be, chastisement, to the king as required.

Historically the balance of power between king and queen mother has turned on character, and there have been times when the *ngwenyama*, or the *ndlovukazi*, has held effective sway. During and after the reign of Mswati, Thandile as queen mother wielded extraordinary power and influence; so, too, did Gwamile later. Sobhuza II, on the other hand, virtually dominated the relationship throughout his reign by the force of his personality and through circumstance.

"Swazi political power," Kuper writes, "radiates primarily from the king."[11] His male relatives, particularly uncles and senior half-brothers, wield great influence. The senior princes are consulted on all important issues; they, among all of his councillors, are also his most forthright critics. As important chiefs or officials themselves, they are also summoned to the capital on vital state occasions rather than residing there semiper-manently, as was once the case. The Swazi also believe that senior princes should not live too close to the royal residence lest they diminish the king's personal or ritual powers. In part to guard against such usurpation, the king is aided by two blood brothers (*tinsila*) chosen from special clans but never Dlamini, as senior officials. Their duties include watching over princes to give guidance and ensure loyalty, and the authority they thus enjoy is equal to that of the most important princes.

Commoners are by no means exluded from governance. Councillors (*tindvuna*) of royal villages placed strategically throughout the country are always commoners, and they exercise a strong influence. They preside over local courts, organize tribute labor, mobilize people for rituals, and act as the eyes and ears of the king. Other commoners serve as minor court officials, age-regiment administrators, and the like. The administrative structure therefore maintains a careful balance between nobility and com-moners in matters of governance. The main motives are first, the king's care not to delegate too much power to kinsmen; and second, the need to utilize the best administrative talent available, irrespective of rank.

The distinction between prince and commoner is maintained in the council structure of the nation. The inner council (*liqoqo*) is an evolution of the Nkosi Dlamini clan council and hence is primarily aristocratic. Membership is small (around thirty) and highly prestigious. Meetings are irregular, called to advise the king on any matter of state importance, and the counsel given is said to be frank, discreet, and influential. In times of succession the *liqoqo* can wield powerful influence in the absence of a strong queen regent. By 1983 it had become evident that the *liqoqo* had taken on extraordinary powers in its (supposedly) advisory role to the queen regent. Some believed that it, not she, was in actual control of events in Swaziland.[12]

The second council, the Swazi national council (*libandla laka Ngwane*, "council of the Ngwane nation"), is by far the more democratic of the two. It includes all prominent chiefs, headmen, councillors, and other able commoners. In fact, the *libandla* is open to any adult male who wishes to attend and to speak, although in practice attendance tends to be self-limiting. The council meets, when summoned, at the cattle byre of the capital, presided over by a prominent *liqoqo* member. The king and queen mother are usually in attendance. Subjects deemed important are discussed, although there is no agenda and no formal rules of parliamentary procedure prevail. Freedom of speech rules, sometimes to a fault, the aim being to prevent factionalism by reaching final agreement on any issue. The idea is that every issue brought to it from the *liqoqo* must be endorsed by the *libandla*, but the outcome is not always as planned.

In times past, the *liqoqo* and the *libandla* were the only means by which the king received public counsel to guide his rule, the true "voices of the people." Those were times when communications were slow and vital issues were not as numerous, complex, or rapidly developing as they are now. From independence to the early 1980s, the national Parliament became the forum for debate over modern issues of governance. During the interregnum after Sobhuza's death, however, events have turned the *liqoqo* into the main policymaking body, with Parliament's powers correspondingly diminished. *Liqoqos* have tried to take on this role in the past, notably following Mswati's death, fortunately without lasting success.

Succession to the Swazi throne is not automatic, although certain traditional guidelines outlining the procedure of the choice are invariably followed. Such a system allows for some flexibility in the case of undesirable qualities in a leading candidate, but it also enables disputes over the succession to arise. These sometimes violent contests have on occasion rendered the nation weak and vulnerable at critical times.

Two underlying factors affect the ambiguity of the succession. First, Swazi nobility for the most part, and the king invariably, remain polygynous. Second, unlike some other peoples, the Swazi do not automatically accept the first wife as the main wife. Particularly in the case of the king, a man will marry one woman according to a ritual that leaves no doubt that she is the main wife and hence the mother of his heir. In the past, kings have followed this procedure late in life, so that the wife might bear a single son and the heir would be too young to challenge his father's powers during the king's lifetime.

But by no means have circumstances always followed the ideal. In every case following the king's death, the formality of convening a special council of immediate kinsmen and the highest notables is followed, and it is their duty (even when the choice is obvious) to name the successor.

Although the king inherits his position from the male line, it is the qualities of his mother, the future queen mother, that are at first the most closely scrutinized. Rank among wives and lineage have in the past been determining factors, although the queen mother is never a Dlamini. In Gwamile's case, force of character and special rainmaking powers overcame her commoner's background to make her the council's choice. The strong tendency is to avoid wives with more than one son, lest fraternal jealousy or the queen mother's favoring of a second son detract from the king's power. Gwamile's reputed preference for her younger son, Malunge, is the best-remembered example of that.

Once the future king is chosen, his raising and training (and in the case of Sobhuza, his education) are matters of foremost importance and are the subject of national attention at every turn. For him, the passage from one growth stage to the next is often heavily ritualized.[13] Since it is often many years before he reaches majority and is installed as king, regents govern in his behalf. Often a previous queen mother or an uncle (or both) have filled this role.

RITUALIZATION OF THE KINGSHIP: THE *INCWALA* CEREMONY

Of greatest significance in the ritualization of the *ngwenyama* is the annual *Incwala* ceremony. Its importance is both symbolic and practical. The king embodies the vitality of the nation. His medicines and powers protect his people from danger and provide for their well-being. His rainmaking powers bring them prosperity. The strength and virility of the king therefore command the constant attention of the nation, and annually it bends itself to their ceremonial renewal.

Of equal practical importance is the *Incwala's* role in reinforcing the legitimacy of the monarchy. This most hallowed ritual, the richest in Swazi symbolism, is the king's alone. He is central to its every facet; when there is no king, there is no *Incwala*. For anyone else to perform the *Incwala* is treason. On two occasions in Swazi history when princes made such attempts, they paid with their lives. It is also a ceremony that sweeps up virtually every significant element in society into performing a specific role in the king's ritualization. Queen mother, queens, princes, councillors, blood brothers, age regiments, ritual specialists, and commoners all have specified duties in the *Incwala* and receive appropriate recognition.

The *Incwala* lasts for roughly three weeks each year, usually during late December or early January, depending on the phase of the moon. There is an element of "first fruit" ceremonial attached to its timing; people are not supposed to consume the new harvest of maize until after the ceremony, but nowadays only the strictest traditionalists seem to adhere to that.

The ceremony itself is lengthy and complex in its symbolism.[14] Several weeks before the ceremony, ritual specialists are sent out to the rivers and to the sea to gather sacred waters, plants, and other potent medicines with which to doctor the king. An initial celebration, days before the major event, takes place in the open cattle byre of the capital, although the principal rites are held in the secrecy of the king's sanctuary. The public participates by performing praise songs and dances commemorating the important events of the kingship. The king spits powerful medicines to the east and the west, symbolizing the renewal of the earth in preparation for the coming growing cycle.

The central ceremony itself lasts six days from the night of the full moon. It is begun by the cutting of branches from sacred trees and their placement surrounding the king's sanctuary in the royal cattle byre by the newest regiment of unmarried youths. It is behind this shield of greenery that the powers of the king are symbolically renewed.

Midway in the ceremony comes the "Day of the Bull," the symbol of potency, during which the king strikes a carefully selected all-black bull with a staff doctored for fertility. The bull is then ritually killed (pummeled to death, in fact, by youths), and its parts are used for medicine and ancestral offerings.

The "Great Day" follows, the climax of the ceremony. In it the king, dressed in his most imposing and symbolic finery, his body gleaming with ointments, consumes the doctored first fruits of the harvest. He is joined by the queen mother and others, after which there is much ritual singing and dancing with carefully specified groups. Finally, the king deftly tosses a green gourd onto the horizontal shield of an agemate; and with the final cleansing of the royal bodies and the burning of the ceremonial objects, the old year is over, the king has renewed his powers, and the nation is prepared for the future.[15]

RELIGION

The traditional religion of the Swazi revolves around the ancestral cult. The spirits of a lineage's ancestor aid the living in coping with the hazards of life—illness, unfaithfulness, crop failure—facilitated by an elaborate system of magic. "The ancestors sanction the desires of their descendants," Kuper asserts; "magic provides the techniques for the achievement of these desires."[16]

The powers of ancestors are believed to be extensive. They do not cause death, but in extreme cases (murder of a kinsman, for instance) they can bar the guilty from access to the spirit world. Ordinarily their influence on the living involves lesser inflictions: bad dreams, sickness, deprivation. There is a hierarchy of spirits, an extension of the rank and prestige of the lineages of the living: hence, the ancestors of the king are regarded as the most powerful of all spirits. So, too, is the sex differentiation among the living carried to the spirit world. Male ancestors stress legal and moral obligations of the living; female spirits guard against harm befalling their kin.

There is no class of priests ordained to deal with ancestral spirits; that duty normally rests with the head of the family. Spirits are appealed to at each significant domestic event—births, marriages, deaths, the moving of homesteads. The king appeals to his ancestors on behalf of his people, again at specified national events, particularly at the *Incwala*, but also during the planting and harvesting of the first main fields, rainmaking, and the like. Propitiation of ancestors is usually accompanied by an offering of beer and meat—and on especially significant occasions, the slaughtering of an ox. Ancestors, Kuper stresses, are not worshipped. "Swazi address them in much the same way as they speak to the living. Their prayers are spontaneous and conversational; they frequently contain rebukes and seldom express gratitude or extreme humility."[17]

In order to successfully interpret and respond to the devices of the spirit world, and to deal with common ailments and other misfortunes, Swazi habitually consult one or both of the main categories of ritual specialists, medicine men (*tinyanga*) and diviners (*tangoma*).

Medicine men are often greatly respected as true professionals, the most successful of them enjoying the highest prestige. Their careers are determined from birth and are believed to be sanctioned by powerful ancestral spirits. Knowledge of rituals and specific medicines is their most highly prized and jealously guarded secret, to be passed on to a single favored son or other preferred relative. Some *tinyanga* are general practitioners; others consider themselves specialists and will treat only a specific illness or misfortune. Their emphasis is on the homeopathic qualities of their proprietary medicines, as distinct from their ritual application, and there is considerable evidence that many of them are very effective. *Tinyanga* are generally (though not exclusively) herbalists, drawing their medicines from trees, roots, and various other natural sources.

Diviners are the more powerful and respected of the specialists. They are in fact regarded with some awe, since they are considered to have been selected by ancestral spirits for their work. Once a man is so possessed, he undergoes long and arduous training by a recognized diviner. *Tangoma* are consulted by individuals with especially troubling or mystifying afflictions or unaccountable misfortunes. Each diviner has his own methods to aid in the diagnosis (bones, rattles, cards, wands) and to indicate the cure. That sometimes involves sacrifices to ancestors, treatment by *tinyanga*, or in extreme cases, the destruction of the witch or sorcerer identified as the source of the trouble.

It is in this latter instance, witchcraft, that ritual practitioners often strain the limits of legality in their therapy. The power of Swazi evildoers (*batsakatsi*) is as firmly believed in as it is feared. Witches, whose power is both physiological and psychological, and sorcerers, who destroy people or property through poisons or violence, are all the more terrifying because their deeds are performed in secret and their identities remain obscured. Evildoers or those who employ them are motivated by fear, jealousy, hatred, or frustrated ambition, so that the victims are most often close relatives, kinsmen, or acquaintances.

Certain diviners specialize in the most challenging and hazardous of all divinations, the "smelling out" of witches and their neutralization or

TABLE 2.5

Swazi Religious Affiliation in 1960

Affiliation	Males (over 18)	Females (over 18)	Total (over 18)
Traditional	50.9	38.6	44.3
Mission churches	28.2	33.3	30.9
Separatist churches	17.4	24.5	21.2
Other Christian	2.7	3.0	2.9
Unknown	0.7	0.6	0.6
Total	99.9%	100.0%	99.9%

Source: J.F. Holleman (ed.), Experiment in Swaziland. Report of the Swaziland Sample Survey 1960 By the Institute for Social Research, University of Natal For the Swaziland Administration (Cape Town: Oxford University Press, 1964).

destruction. Since, of all practices of the occult, both witchcraft and sorcery (and their antidotes) are the most likely to involve violence and death, their exercise has long been outlawed. But their occult practice, although impossible to measure, continues by all accounts to increase among a people haunted by feelings of helplessness and inadequacy in a complex and threatening world.[18]

Although the Swazi do not worship nature gods, there is a definite ritual association between the monarchy and certain natural phenomena. The king is identified with the sun, and his male kinship line is referred to as the *mlangeni* ("people of the sun").[19] Above all, rain is believed to be controlled by medicines in the exclusive control of the dyarchy—the *ngwenyama* and the *ndlovukazi*. Throughout southern Africa, Swazi rulers have enjoyed legendary fame as rainmakers, the most renowned of all being Gwamile.[20] The special medicines employed are of course closely guarded secrets, but they are said to include consecrated river water and portions of pregnant animals, together with the most precious element, the rain stone, which is kept secluded at the capital. Absence of rain, occasioning royal intervention, is commonly laid to the anger of royal ancestors over popular disobedience, to the breach of taboos, or to other transgressions. Belief in the rainmaking powers of the rulers is among the firmest of popular convictions. In times of prolonged drought, European farmers have joined in the requests to the king to bring rain.

Traditional religion, whether open or occult, has been increasingly subjected to challenge by Christianity during this century. The Wesleyans established their first mission in southern Swaziland in the 1840s, followed by the Anglicans in the 1870s, the German Lutherans in the 1880s, and the South African (Dutch Reformed) and Scandinavian Alliance missions in the 1890s. The Roman Catholics arrived in 1914, and in the 1920s the American Nazarene Mission established a major presence in Swaziland, creating churches, schools, and health facilities, most notably the Raleigh

TABLE 2.6

Swazi Christian Affiliation in 1960 (Over 18) By Denomination

Affiliation	Percentages
Methodist	25.1
Evangelical Alliance Mission	14.9
Anglican	12.3
Nazarene	9.1
Apostolic Faith Mission	7.2
Apostolic Holy Catholic Church in Zion	6.4
Roman Catholic	5.3
Christian Apostolic Zulu Church in Zion	4.2
Swedish Alliance Mission	3.8
Swazi Christian Church in Zion	2.7
United Christian Church in Africa	1.7
South African General Mission	1.5
African Methodist Episcopalian (A.M.E.)	1.1
Berlin Lutheran	1.1
Seventh Day Adventist	1.0
Other Christian	2.6
Total	100.0%

Source: J. F. Holleman (ed.), Experiment in Swaziland. Report of the Swaziland Sample Survey 1960 By the Institute for Social Research, University of Natal For the Swaziland Administration (Cape Town: Oxford University Press, 1964).

Fitkin hospital in Manzini. The challenge to traditional spiritualism by Christianity can be seen in the rise in the number of adherents over the past sixty years. In 1921, 4 percent of the Swazi population was listed as Christian. By 1946 the figure had risen to 35 and by 1956 to 60 percent, before leveling off (See Table 2.5).[21]

Twenty-four recognized Christian missions now operate in Swaziland, contributing in one form or another not only evangelization through churches, newspapers, and radio, but also to education and to health care. Since the 1930s, however, growing numbers of Swazi converts have been drawn toward independent or separatist sects, which are characterized by exclusively black pastorates and worship services that to a greater or lesser degree combine Christian dogma and liturgy with traditional custom. Some white churches, notably the Catholic Church, have made eclectic responses to these sectarian challenges, with some success; but the separatist movement, with its nationalistic overtones, continues to experience a surge of popularity. This has been particularly true of the various Zionist denominations, stemming perhaps from the public support given to the Zionist Separatist church by the *ndlovukazi*, Lomawa, in the 1930s.[22]

THE WORK CYCLE AND THE DIVISION OF LABOR

As Swaziland remains largely agricultural, the cycles and the divisions of work that dominate life are those that prevail in the countryside. Mixed farming is predominant in the rural economy, the main subsistence crops being maize (corn, or "mealies" in Swazi parlance) and millet, the stock being cattle, supplemented by goats and to a lesser extent sheep. Hunting and gathering are still pursued, although not nearly as extensively as in former times.

Life consequently follows the rhythm of the seasons. Spring plowing and sowing get under way with the arrival of the rains in September. If the summer rains fall as heavily as expected, successive plantings may be staggered all the way through January. Family and communal work parties, predominantly women and children, are commonly seen working and weeding the fields during summer. In autumn (February and March), women harvest the grain and it is carried home for processing. In winter, from April to July, the maize is removed from the cobs, and the millet threshed and winnowed and then consumed or reserved for storage. Millet is brewed into beer as a reward for communal work, and harvest time and early winter are consequently the times for social conviviality and family get-togethers. Festivities are the occasions when the traditional starchy fare is supplemented with meat and milk, both prized, especially in combination. Although meat is consumed more regularly these days, the slaughter of a beast remains a festive occasion. Fall and winter, being dry and lightning-free, are also the times for the building of huts and the repair of thatched roofs. Stock herding, of course, goes on year round.

Nowadays wage employment, either local or migrant, allows for the rounding out of the subsistence diet with purchased foodstuffs. There are butcheries in even the smallest settlements, and there is a well-developed national distribution system for ground maize, bread, and packaged milk. Drought still brings hardship, but rarely the hunger or even starvation of former times.

Division of agricultural labor depends on sex, age, and to some degree, rank. Men plow, build, and tend the cattle. Women attend to domestic chores, cooking, grinding grain, fetching wood and water. They also maintain the house, once built, repairing thatch and smearing floors with cow dung. For some, another normal duty of weaving mats and baskets has turned into a cash-generating cottage industry for the tourist trade. Women are also responsible for cultivation and weeding and, along with the entire family, harvesting. When one adds to this their primary responsibility for the raising of the children, there is no question that Swazi women bear the greater burden of the continuous and monotonous tasks necessary for the maintenance of daily existence.

Children, as they grow older, are expected to participate in family tasks, particularly fieldwork. Girls take over certain domestic responsibilities, and boys tend and herd the stock. That teaches them responsibility, for the lad who loses a family beast to theft or collision by a car, or allows a mealie field to be trampled, will not soon forget the consequences.

Chiefs and other nobility are exceptions to normal work patterns. Although they do not escape physical work, their fields and herds are

Herdboys with dog in the middleveld near Luyengo. Photo by the author.

likely to be extensive, so that tribute labor in a more or less feudal manner is the custom. Those who *khonta* (pay homage to) a chief sow, cultivate, and harvest his fields from time to time. Food, beer, and meat are provided by the chief on these occasions; and of course it is never forgotten that it is the chief who controls the allocation of the commoners' lands.

As in so many areas, modern ways have modified tradition in varying degrees in rural life. Women, for instance, were once forbidden to tend, or even approach, cattle. But now, with the men absent on migrant labor, women can be seen occasionally plowing the fields behind teams of oxen, and the sight of a young girl herding cattle is quite common. Migration has also had its effect on tribute labor: Now it is often acceptable for a man away at harvest time to make a contribution to his chief in cash, grain, or small-stock instead of appearing for work.

DISTRIBUTION OF WEALTH

In rural Swaziland, a man's wealth is still measured in cattle, women, and children. Land, where it can be purchased in title deed, affords more wealth and status. For the vast majority, however, land remains out of reach from individual ownership. Men by birth have the right, once they are married, to the use of plots adequate for their needs in the districts of their forefathers' chiefs. Grazing, firewood, thatching grass, and fencing reeds are available to all. But conspicuous improvement of the land, or innovation in its use, is frowned upon by the more conservative chiefs, and the man who fences his fields, uses modern fertilizing or irrigation methods, or even grows cash crops without the prior approval of the chief is taking a risk. In rare instances, people have been removed from such lands. To the extent that Swazi Nation Land constitutes wealth, therefore, it is communal, not individual; and it is not husbanded and improved as is individually tenured land. Many believe that this is the ultimate cause of Swazi underproductivity. Whether or not that is so, the visible difference between the condition and productivity of typical Swazi Nation Land and title deed land owned or contracted for by Swazi individuals is dramatic and moving.

Today, as formerly, a man's wives and his children are indications of his wealth and prestige, although the correlation between numbers and economic value is far more obscure. In the past, when wealth was derived exclusively from agricultural surplus, numerous wives and numbers of children were translatable through labor into greater harvests. Now, with incomes derived more and more from wages, multiple families, like the great English estates of yesteryear, have often become prohibitively expensive to maintain. As with those estates, prestige accrues to polygynous men because they are demonstrably able to afford several wives, not because the wives themselves are any longer sources of wealth. Children in modern times remain potential sources of wealth to the degree that they are educated and hence have access to wealth-producing jobs. Student positions at the nation's better secondary schools and at the University of Swaziland are highly prized and keenly sought after.

Today, therefore, the greatest store of wealth in rural Swaziland remains cattle. Their value is multifaceted. First, there is nothing about cattle that is not somehow useful. Their meat, milk, hides, horns, and manure are all usable or consumable. Their blood and bones can be processed into fertilizer. Second, they are a very prudent investment. With proper care and luck, the owner of a head or two can increase them to a herd within a few years. Since grazing is communal, overhead (aside from veterinary costs) is minimal.[23] It is said that the gross return on a herd of Swazi cattle, with any luck, can run to 25 percent per annum. Cattle are nearly as liquid as cash; few if any banks in Swaziland will not accept them as loan collateral. Finally, the ritual value of cattle, and the prestige connected with their ownership, are without parallel. Cattle are the medium for propitiating ancestors and are the currency of legitimate marriage (*lobola*). Their presence is required for every significant family and national ritual. Parts of them are used ritually in doctoring the ill and in bringing on abundance and prosperity. A man who owns a large herd is considered blessed indeed; one without cattle is said to be "an orphan without kin."[24]

SOCIAL CHANGE AND CLASS DIFFERENTIATION

The social structure of rural life and the political system that controls it is still predominate in present-day Swaziland. But this way of life has undergone great change as the result of the powerful and diverse challenges of the past hundred years. Swaziland, though small, is deeply involved in the outside world, both economically and politically—to a far greater degree, one senses, than is comfortable for many. The challenges will continue, and the degree to which Swazi citizens and their leadership can adapt to further change while remaining true to their traditions will in great measure determine the character of their future. The final portion of this chapter, and much of the remainder of this volume, will discuss the nature of these stresses and the character of the Swazi response.

Essentially, the dilemma Swaziland faces is typical of every country in the developing world. An agricultural economy finds itself under the pressures of international capitalism, to which it will either adjust (at a cost to social stability and tradition) or not (ultimately at greater cost). This is nothing new: For the last hundred years, since the concessionaires appeared at Mbandzeni's capital, the stresses have been there. Cattle disease introduced (inadvertently) by the Boers and the imposition of European taxes made migrant laborers out of Swazi warriors and cultivators. The expropriation of the land quickened the process, and the influx of capital after World War II began a socio-economic transformation of the homestead from which there was no turning back.

Since early in this century, the prudent homestead head has responded to the new realities and has often prospered in doing so. He has earned enough wages locally or in South Africa to pay his taxes and secure his future. Typically, wages have first purchased cattle to *lobola* a wife and to achieve independence from the father's homestead. They have subsequently improved crop productivity through the purchase of plows and oxen and, more recently, through tractor hire. They have finally been invested in the migrant's children in the form of school fees, for it is common wisdom that the surest path to advancement is through education.

Since "advancement" means jobs in the city, the flow of educated and semieducated job seekers to the urban areas of Swaziland has been the most significant and most perplexing social phenomenon confronting the authorities since World War II. In spite of all efforts to control and modify it, the urban migration grows daily. So does the migration of the uneducated from the homestead to the cane fields, the canneries, and the sawmills of Swaziland. And the reason in each case is that "tradition" no longer makes economic sense. Wages more than make up for the maize shortfall caused by the migrant's absence; with any luck the surplus cash brought home might buy a cow. Mine wages in South Africa are many times what a man can earn cutting sugarcane in Mhlume or Big Bend. Who would not leave the farming to the family and go off for that?

Science building at the University of Swaziland, Kwaluseni campus. Photo by the author.

As was true in all parts of colonial Africa, the value of education as the surest means to upward mobility was recognized very early on in Swaziland. Mission schools, first primary and then secondary, were the earliest to be established, and places in them were coveted. But it was not only the missions that created that impetus. The keen national interest in the education of the young king (on whom the citizenry was counting to win back the land), the founding of the royal school at Zombodze and his dispatch to Lovedale, all focused attention on the need for education. Sobhuza himself always reinforced this need and stressed the value of education to his people. He opened the first Swazi national high school at Matsapha in 1931, just as he dedicated the University College of Swaziland in 1973.

Added to these incentives from missions and royalty were the material rewards to be derived from an education, discernible to all. By the late 1950s, 92 percent of those completing secondary education were employed in the cities; of those with no education remaining in the countryside, less than half found wage-earning jobs. In the cities, employed secondary school-leavers earned on average two and one-half times the salaries of those without an education. So the numbers of males completing secondary education (standard seven) were more than double in 1959 what they had been in 1940.[25]

Following independence in 1968, the government placed heavy emphasis on mass education. Its goals were ambitious. "It is the right of every child to have access to education," asserted the *Third National Development Plan* (1977).[26] Its goal was to achieve universal primary (seven-year) education by 1985, and eventually a nationwide junior secondary

TABLE 2.7

Enrollments and Teachers in Swaziland's Primary and Secondary Schools

Year	Number of Schools	Number of Pupils	Number of Teachers
i) Primary Schools			
1968	358	62,082	1,627
1973	395	81,694	2,112
1974	403	86,110	2,220
1975	412	89,528	2,363
1976	420	92,721	2,513
1977	436	96,835	2,672
1978	436	100,700	2,853
1979	440	105,607	3,016
1980	450	112,019	3,278
% Increase since 1968	25.7	80.4	101.5
% Increase since 1973	13.9	37.1	55.2
ii) Secondary Schools			
1968	31	3,792	232
1973	64	12,459	550
1974	66	14,301	611
1975	67	16,227	739
1976	67	17,396	885
1977	70	19,359	978
1978	76	20,584	1,073
1979	81	22,091	1,158
1980	82	23,198	1,292
% Increase since 1968	164.5	511.8	456.9
% Increase since 1973	28.1	86.2	134.9

Source: Swaziland Government, Central Statistical Office, Annual Statistical Bulletin, 1968, 1977, 1978, 1979, 1980.

(ten-year) program. School construction was accelerated, as were the capacities of the two existing teacher training colleges (William Pitcher and Nazarene) and the new one at Nhlangano. The University College at Kwaluseni and Luyengo was scheduled to increase its capacity significantly to meet national manpower needs, particularly in the sciences and the professions. Much was accomplished during the postindependence decade, particularly at the secondary level: Between 1968 and 1977 the number of schools more than doubled, and more than four times the number of teachers taught almost five times as many students (see Table 2.7).

TABLE 2.8

Teacher Qualifications, Swaziland's Primary and Secondary Schools

Year	Qualified	Unqualified	Total	% Qualified
i) Primary Schools				
1968	1,176	451	1,627	72.3
1973	1,618	494	2,112	76.6
1974	1,643	577	2,220	74.0
1975	1,644	719	2,363	69.6
1976	1,699	814	2,513	67.6
1977	1,978	694	2,672	74.0
1978	2,194	659	2,853	76.9
1979	2,442	574	3,016	81.0
1980	2,203	493	2,696	81.7
% Increase since 1968	87.3	9.3	65.7	13.0
% Increase since 1973	36.1	0.0	27.7	6.7
ii) Secondary Schools				
1968	274	26	300	91.3
1973	467	83	550	84.9
1974	480	131	611	78.6
1975	538	201	739	72.8
1976	655	230	885	74.0
1977	741	237	978	75.8
1978	811	262	1,073	75.6
1979	908	250	1,158	78.4
1980	992	300	1,292	76.8
% Increase since 1968	262.0	1053.8	330.7	(15.9)
% Increase since 1973	112.4	261.5	134.9	(9.5)

Source: Swaziland Government, Central Statistical Office, Annual Statistical Bulletin, 1968, 1977, 1978, 1979, 1980.

The numbers, as impressive as some of them were, disappointed the planners. They never kept up with population growth; yet even the pace that was set clearly strained the system's capacity to maintain quality. Teacher qualification levels decreased "dangerously" during the mid-1970s at both the primary and secondary levels (see Table 2.8), and the Education Ministry's fears of jeopardizing student results were fully realized. By 1977, first and second-class "O-level" pass rates were less than half what

59

TABLE 2.9

Swaziland Student Examination Results: 'O-Level' Certificate

Year	En-trants	1st Class Pass	1st Class %	2nd Class Pass	2nd Class %	3rd Class Pass	3rd Class %	4th Class Pass	4th Class %	Fail	Fail %
1968	240	33	13.7	61	25.4	86	35.8	(n)	(n)	60	25.0
1973	806	44	5.5	84	10.4	195	24.2	307	38.1	176	21.8
1974	1,037	59	5.7	105	10.1	228	22.0	392	37.8	253	24.4
1975	1,120	56	5.0	111	9.9	248	22.1	450	40.2	255	22.8
1976	1,251	58	4.6	140	11.2	278	22.2	733	58.6	42	3.4
1977	1,432	79	5.5	115	8.0	283	19.8	837	58.5	118	8.2
1978	1,705	76	4.5	148	8.7	312	18.3	1,008	59.1	161	9.4
1979	1,707	95	5.6	165	9.7	327	19.2	1,061	62.2	59	3.4
1980	1,833	90	4.9	208	11.3	362	19.8	1,114	60.8	59	3.2
% In-crease since 1968	663.8	172.7	(64.2)	241.0	(55.5)	320.9	(44.7)	(n)	(n)	(1.7)	(681.2)
% In-crease since 1973	127.4	104.5	(10.9)	147.6	(8.7)	85.6	(18.2)	262.9	59.6	(66.5)	(581.2)

Source: Swaziland Government, Central Statistical Office, Annual Statistical Bulletin, 1968, 1977, 1978, 1979, 1980.

(n) = not available

they had been in 1968, and the fourth-class rates increased (see Table 2.9).[27] By 1982 the overall pass rate had dropped to one entrant in four. New approaches as well as renewed efforts were required before the government could begin to achieve its goals of achieving quality, as well as quantity, in education.

Still, the educational establishment that had developed since World War II had produced school-leavers in sufficient numbers by the 1980s to have formed a new and significant class that is today in all senses an elite. It is educated, ambitious, affluent, and aware of its status and political power. It has permeated all levels of the government bureaucracy and the civil service, but to date it has not succeeded in passing through mid-level in the management of the multinational corporations. The government, responding to middle-class frustration over this failure, reinforced daily by the visible affluence of the European managerial class from which the Swazi middle class is excluded, has made periodic attempts to Africanize these businesses faster than the targeted companies consider prudent. In Janurary 1982 the Kirsh-owned Metro Wholesale enterprise announced its closure after the government attempted to localize its upper management by refusing to renew the work permits of one or two of its expatriate managers. The government backed down, but the incident highlighted the continuing dilemma of its highest officials in meeting the need to maintain an attractive investment climate for foreign capital while responding to the mounting pressures of a growing and increasingly impatient domestic elite.

The emergence of the new Swazi elite has heightened class tensions with another privileged group as well. During this century there was created a community of Eurafricans ("coloureds"), largely the offspring of Swazi women and white settlers or officials. As of 1976 they numbered only about 4,000 or less than 1 percent of the population.[28] But true to British imperial tradition, the coloureds had been accorded highly privileged status during the colonial years, which had given them power and prominence out of all proportion to their numbers. Separate schools, trading licenses in areas forbidden to blacks, and other favored treatment had, by the time of independence, fostered a Eurafrican middle class that was both wealthy and aggressively aware of its status.

Consequently, in 1968 Swazi resentment at alleged coloured clannishness and profiteering no longer had a colonial buffer between it and the object of its frustrations. Since then, tensions between black and coloured have been if anything heightened by the actions of the Swazi bureaucracy. Through one technicality or another, few Eurafricans have been granted full Swazi citizenship, including passports. In recent years the government has introduced (but not passed) legislation that would require Swazi parentage through the male line as a requirement for qualification as a citizen.[29] Swazi employees' associations, notably the bank employees' union, have complained bitterly at the favoritism that allegedly continues to be extended to coloured management. Consequently, although

Eurafricans remain a highly prominent element in Swazi business and professional circles, the clash of elites since independence has made their continued legal and political status in the country of their birth a matter of continuing doubt and concern.

Analyzing the essence of a major social movement, such as class formation, in a few sentences is at best hazardous. But if one can judge from the recent past, the new Swazi middle class seems to be more aggressive economically than politically. Its immediate frustrations stem from its continuing perception that it is restricted from access to the truly remunerative and prestigious top management positions. Likewise, without special connections in high circles, it is hardly possible to obtain the credit and licensing necessary to establish the really profitable businesses, such as bottle (liquor) stores. Land ownership also remains out of reach of all but the most affluent and influential. And the middle class knows that too much of the country's wealth is being exported—legally or otherwise—by foreign-owned enterprise, leaving too little for local reinvestment and development. Teachers in particular continue to feel unrecognized and underpaid. The dismal 0-level pass rate of less than 27 percent in 1982 reflects, as much as anything, the collapse of teacher morale.

Yet the political turmoil, often violence, that has accompanied similar processes of class formation and differentiation in other African countries has only briefly threatened the political order in Swaziland. Since 1973 (1977, in the case of the teachers), opposition parties and unions have not challenged government restrictions to any significant degree. In the countryside the chiefs, who have inevitably lost power and status as the locus of activity has shifted toward city and industry, have accommodated. They have maintained their feudal positions, and they have ensured their children's education. The stresses between the old and the new elites that have so afflicted the postindependence histories of Ghana and Nigeria have in Swaziland been contained. The king's entrenchment of the ruling class by suspending the constitution in 1973 was in part responsible, but that could not have been done peaceably amongst a citizenry more radicalized. And for all the elite's frustrations, the fact remains that its relations with the European bourgeoisie have been peaceful and essentially cooperative since independence. Africanization of the public and private sectors, it must be added, has outpaced that in other countries in the region, notably Botswana.

The period following the death of the *ngwenyama* will be a time of testing for the Swazi middle class. For although the forces of conservatism won out in the early 1970s, the issues that produced the social activism of those years remain. The banning of the Ngwane National Liberatory Congress (NNLC) suppressed the middle-class aspirations that provided much of its support, but it did not dissolve them. At the beginning of the 1980s the main economic concern of many middle-class Swazi refocused on an issue that had given rise to much of the opposition of the early 1970s, public ownership of the means of production. Many in government have become concerned over the rapid amassing of wealth and power by the Tibiyo Taka Ngwane Fund, which, controlled by the king in trust for the nation but independent of parliamentary scrutiny and immune from taxation, seemed to many to have taken on a sort of statehood of its own. The clash between government and Tibiyo bureaucracies that many have anticipated surfaced briefly in 1982, when each launched its own feasibility study for the development of the last great irrigable river basin remaining in the country. The issue was apparently resolved, but many observers saw in it an indication of the character and the form that future struggles between the forces of traditionalism and modernism were likely to take in the post-Sobhuza era.

3

Government and Politics, 1963–1983

THE INDEPENDENCE DECADE, 1963–1973

Swaziland became an independent nation in September 1968. Events leading to its independence extended back to the end of World War II, when it became increasingly evident that South Africa's racial policies precluded the kingdom's transfer to the Union. Following the 1948 Nationalist victory in the Union, the British implemented a series of measures aimed at devolving power to a systematized local administration in Swaziland. By the early 1960s that process in the kingdom (as in much of British Africa, the exceptions being South Africa and Southern Rhodesia) was in full swing. Steps were taken in 1962 and 1963 to form an interim Legislative Council (from members of the Swazi National Council and the European Advisory Council) and to write a constitution preparatory to the granting of independence.

Political events from the early 1960s onward were dominated by the struggles between the various classes and interest groups that had emerged as the century progressed. It is worthwhile therefore to examine briefly the character of the three major domestic groupings involved: the monarchy, the European settlers, and the Swazi petite bourgeoisie.

Sobhuza and his predecessor Gwamile had greatly strengthened the position of the monarchy in traditional society. With skill, guile, and decisiveness, they both had parlayed a colonial disposition to employ a carefully circumscribed royal establishment in its scheme of indirect rule into a position of power and prestige beyond anything calculated by the colonials. But by no means, as the country moved toward independence, was the paramountcy of the monarchy assured. White settlers held nearly half the land—and virtually all of the developed and irrigated acreage— in freehold. Through the European Advisory Council and the various farmers' organizations they had wielded powerful influence in the colonial state since the 1920s. Their determination to remain predominant after

King Sobhuza II at the opening of Parliament, 8 April 1971. Photo from the Swaziland National Archives.

independence was obvious. Another rival was the emerging Swazi elite, independent of the royal line, produced by the educational system and the rapidly developing economy, which was determined to secure and to enhance its distinct position.

The monarchy's strengths were considerable. Both Gwamile and Sobhuza had enhanced its prestige by standing up to the colonials with courage and determination. The *ngwenyama* by the 1960s had undeniably become a charismatic figure (he was believed to be an admirer of General de Gaulle).[1] Sobhuza's powers were enhanced to no small degree by his skillful use of the elaborate annual rituals that served to reinforce the legitimacy of the monarchy. But the source of the royal house's greatest strength by far was its control of Swazi Nation Land (SNL). That land, the bulk of which had been the former Native Areas, as added to by the various Lifa Fund and colonial purchases, comprised over half of Swaziland's acreage by 1968. It was held by the king in the traditional manner "in trust for the nation"; that is, it was distributed to the people in usufruct only through the chiefs, placing a premium on loyalty to them, and through them to the king. There was consequently a strong politico-economic rationale for the king's heavy emphasis on "traditionalism" throughout his lifetime. What limited the *ngwenyama's* power most of all was his lack of access to the mineral wealth underneath the soil, which remained in the hands of the colonial state and its European beneficiaries.

The power of the European settlers lay in their lands. Their power had been considerably increased by the massive influx of development capital following the war, in the benefits of which they had shared disproportionately (notably the irrigation schemes of the 1950s, aimed largely at improving freehold lands). Their interests lay in their continued dominance of the relations of production in the areas they controlled. Throughout the twentieth century their interests had consequently rivaled those of the monarchy, which had sought to return the lands to Swazi control. Settler interests had consistently won out over the monarchy in the continuing struggle for colonial administrative patronage.

The Swazi petite bourgeoisie, whose roots lay in the beginning of the colonial era, became a discernible interest group in the years following World War II. It was a product of the government-sponsored education system, the initial graduates of which became for the most part teachers, clerks, and minor civil servants, to which were added a number of traders, smallholders, and artisans. With the passage of years, as it both grew and matured as a differentiated class, it gradually became conscious of its interests as distinct not only from those of the settlers (which had always been the case), but from those of the traditional elite (royal house and chiefs) as well. The interests of the petite bourgeoisie lay in securing and improving its separate position (especially wages and conditions) within the modernizing postwar society. In the political struggles of the 1960s and 1970s its representative political parties claimed to speak for the Swazi working class as well as its own interests, which made them an even more ominous threat in the eyes of both the monarchy and the settlers.

Those were the general alignments vying to secure their interests as the colonial state moved to transfer power in the early 1960s. Two constitutional conferences were held in London during 1962 and 1963, the second of them bringing together politicians and notables from the Swazi, European, and Eurafrican communities as the Swazi delegation. Both convenings ended in failure. The contentious issues centered on the constitutional power of the king, the vesting of the country's mineral rights, and the method of electing the Legislative Council members. As a result, Britain put forward its own constitutional proposal in May 1963. It was an act of great consequence, chiefly because its major provisions, seen by both the monarchy and the settlers as inimical to their interests, brought about a coalescing of those two forces, whose interests had historically been at odds.

The constitution, which the British placed in force in 1964, gave even greater executive powers to the "queen's commissioner" than the colonial resident commissioner had ever held. Those included the continued vesting of all mineral rights and revenues, which the king was demanding for the Swazi nation, in the colonial state. The commissioner likewise retained sufficient appointive power over the new Legislative Council to keep it free from domination by either the king or the settlers (although each was assured substantial power on the council through separate voters' rolls). Furthermore, a full third of the council's elected membership was to be democratically chosen. So under the 1964 constitution, king and settler stood to lose power to the colonial government and to the Swazi petite bourgeoisie; and in opposition to the constitution, king and settler solidified an alliance.[2]

Elections to the Legislative Council were held in June 1964, in an atmosphere of royal (and hence, to a large degree, popular) and settler hostility to their constitutional basis. The climate was galvanized by the fact of the emergency and the British army occupation (see Chapter 1), which had been brought about by the labor agitation of 1963. Within this ferment, political parties, which had formed in anticipation of independence as far back as 1960, now realigned themselves and adjusted their positions in the election campaign. Three principal parties emerged, each broadly representing one of the class interests described above.

The monarchy (the king and the Swazi National Council, the chiefs, and the nobility) had traditionally commanded the loyalty of the peasantry on Swazi Nation Land. Two months prior to the election, in April 1964, the monarchy formed its own political arm, the Imbokodvo National Movement (INM). Its aims included training programs and agricultural improvements to benefit the peasantry. But the INM's main purpose was to ensure the reproduction of the monarchy through the preservation of its traditional tenure of the land in the precapitalist sector and through the acquisition of control over all mineral resources to be relinquished by the colonial administration at independence.[3]

The European settler element, now a strongly developing bourgeoisie, formed the United Swaziland Association (USA). Its aim was to preserve the political and economic interests of the Europeans, which had been effectively looked after by the European Advisory Council since 1921. It was specifically determined to protect property rights as they had existed since the 1907 Proclamation against the possibility of nationalization by an independent government.

The interests of the Swazi petite bourgeoisie commanded the attention of several parties,[4] but the 1964 election eliminated all but one as a serious political force. That was the Ngwane National Liberatory Congress, whose concerns centered on the furtherance of middle-class Swazi interests, as against those of the Swazi nobility and the Europeans. The NNLC espoused gains for labor through union organization, and training for and localization of middle-level and supervisory positions in both the public and private sectors. It also stood, notably, for the vesting of both land and minerals in a representative governmental system.

It was during the 1964 election that the *ngwenyama* demonstrated his consummate skills as a modern, Western-style politician. Indeed, the four-year period between the election campaign and the achievement of independence was the time when the king exhibited most dramatically the extent of his political shrewdness and pragmatic skills, the result of which was the legitimation of royal dominance. It was, for him and his interests, a political *tour de force.*

It all seemed to get off, however, to an inauspicious start. The king in early 1964 held a plebiscite in order to demonstrate popular opposition to the imposed constitution and thus to prevent an election. By any standard, the result was a massive popular endorsement of the *ngwenyama's* position; of over 122,000 Swazi voters, only 154 voted for the constitution. Yet the British ignored the vote and proceeded with the constitution's implementation.[5]

But the king had dramatically demonstrated his popularity and power over the peasantry, and it was at that point that he hastily formed the INM and joined the political battle within the framework of the constitution. The election results confirmed the previous indications of the plebiscite. The INM garnered 85 percent of the vote, and Sobhuza's supporters won all of the Swazi seats. Of the opposition parties, only the NNLC scored any success (12 percent of the vote); the others slipped into oblivion, their leadership for the most part joining the INM or otherwise falling into line with the king.

So too did the 1964 election point up the growing symbiosis between the settlers and the monarchy. The king since 1960 had made clear his intention of preserving existing property rights, an assurance repeated in the INM platform, which called for the "creation . . . of a favourable climate for outside capital investment." The USA for its part gave its official support to the king's long-standing claim to his undivided control, in trust for the nation, over land and minerals.[6] Significantly, Carl Todd, a leading European planter and entrepreneur, won his seat as an INM member, while six out of the remaining seven "white" seats went to the USA.

The *ngwenyama's* decision to join the 1964 election fight rather than to boycott it was clearly a turning point in his solidification of royal power. Imbokodvo won a smashing victory, as did the USA, the party in support of the king's land and mineral claims, among the settlers. The Swazi opposition emerged from the election in disarray, with only the NNLC still viable. "The creation of the Imbokodvo National Movement," one analyst observed, "dramatically altered the political situation in Swaziland; it gave the traditionalists a vehicle by which they could challenge the political parties on their own terms but with the power and prestige of the monarchy solidly behind them."[7]

Now the king turned to the question of the constitution. The fact that he had won under its provisions did nothing to lessen his mistrust or his dislike of it. In his campaign to redraft it, Sobhuza was aided by a bit of luck. In March 1964 the queen's commissioner, Sir Brian Marwick, was replaced. Marwick had consistently opposed the desires of king and settler in favor of a one-man, one-vote constitution, and had remained hostile to the vesting of minerals in the king. His successor was Francis (later Sir Francis) Loyd, a man who proved to be more solicitous in every way of the furthering of the *ngwenyama's* aims.

In 1965 the Loyd administration granted the Imbokodvo request for a commission to draw up an independence constitution to replace the 1964 document. The composition of that body itself was a victory for the king; it was chaired by Loyd and consisted of INM and USA members exclusively. No opposition (NNLC) member was allowed to sit on the panel.

The constitution that emerged from this body constituted a triumph for the new monarchy-settler alliance. The document was adapted from the British parliamentary model, but under its provisions the Swazi king was to be no Westminster-style constitutional monarch with little actual power. One-fifth of the thirty-member Assembly were to be his nominees; the remaining twenty-four were to be elected by a universal franchise from eight three-member constituencies. Those constituencies were weighted toward the rural sector, where the king's political strength was centered. He was also to choose half of the twelve-member Senate, the upper house of Parliament, which could delay but not block legislation. The king would appoint as well the chief justice and the prime minister, the latter on the basis of a parliamentary majority. The prime minister, along with the rest of the cabinet, served in an advisory capacity to the *ngwenyama*.

Most important in the light of subsequent events, the new constitution provided a powerful and secure capital base for the reproduction of the monarchy along traditional lines. It thus provided the fulfillment of a primary goal of the king since his coronation in 1921. By its terms, the *ngwenyama's* tenure over SNL lands (but not, of course, over European-owned freehold lands) was reaffirmed. More important, the constitution also vested the ownership and revenue of all minerals in the king, not (as the NNLC and Marwick had sought) in the new parliamentary government. That was a signal victory for the royal house, and it would be a key factor in the character of the postindependence development of the country.[8]

Those years (1964–1967) were also notable politically as the period when the USA withered away as a political force, a development that must be viewed in concert with the solidification of the king's power. It declined partly because the realization of its primary goal, the securing of settler relations of production by the king's repeated assurances, made its continuation as an active political force somewhat superfluous. But in part the USA's demise came because of a falling-out with Imbokodvo over the issue of voter's rolls under the new constitution, a battle the USA lost. All during the deliberations it had held out for its long-standing goal of seats reserved for Europeans, but in the end the INM won a single national roll. The INM-USA split, and Imbokodvo's victory, in fact signaled the final triumph of the king's quest for political paramountcy. They indicated the INM's cool calculation that after its smashing 1964 victory, USA backing was thenceforth desirable but not indispensable. The USA's angry response to this seeming betrayal was tempered by the king's reassurance about the continuance of existing property relations. By 1966 the USA, the settlers' public policy arm, was a spent force, and the king's political victory was complete.

The new constitution was promulgated in February 1967, and it became the basis for the independence election, held the following April. Its results at once confirmed the solidification of royal power and at the same time indicated the source of future political strife. For the INM (now with strong settler backing) won every seat in the new Parliament, polling over 75 percent of the vote in seven out of the eight constituencies. But in the Mphumalanga constituency, which included the Vuvulane Irrigated Farms scheme and the Mhlume and Big Bend sugar complexes, the NNLC demonstrated its strong appeal among urban and industrial voters. There it garnered 47 percent of the vote. But even those numbers were not sufficient to win any seats, and the NNLC thus remained an opposition party without a voice in Parliament.[9]

On 25 April 1967 Sobhuza was officially installed as king of the new constitutional state. Fifteen months later, on 6 September 1968, he received the instruments of government, marking Swaziland's independence. Sobhuza had become a notable exception to the trend then prevailing in Africa, where most kings lost, not gained, political power with the independence of their states.[10] He did so by skillfully and shrewdly taking on the Europeans (officials and settlers) in a Western-style political power struggle and beating them at their own game. He also succeeded in neutralizing the Swazi opposition, but that victory proved to be more ephemeral. Decisive action outside the provisions of the constitution would prove necessary before that obstacle to royal paramountcy was permanently suppressed.

The first five years of independence were, politically speaking, a time of settling in and adjusting to the new realities and alignments, both for the government and the opposition—a period, in other words, not untypical of any newly independent African country. The NNLC underwent a power struggle, centering on Dr. Ambrose Zwane's attempts to entrench his power permanently in opposition to the wishes of the younger leadership. The government, too, witnessed the beginnings of a polarization between the "traditionalists" and the "modernizers," the spokesmen for the former being the prime minister and leader of the INM, Prince Makhosini Dlamini, and the minster for local administration, Prince Mfanasibili Dlamini. Two younger rising stars of the political establishment, whose modern views set them apart, were Simon Sishayi Nxumalo (minister of commerce, industry, and mines), an early defector from the opposition to the king's political movement, and Zonke Khumalo (deputy prime minister), one of whose wives was a favorite daughter of the king.

The new government turned mainly to the two issues that were the principal concerns of a burgeoning and increasingly demanding petite bourgeoisie, land and the Africanization (or localization) of the bureaucracy and of lower management in the private sector. Of the two, localization was the less ambiguous and most politically popular class issue. The government committed itself to a militant policy of indigenization. The king established two localization committees, one for the public and the other for the private sector, to hasten the process, consistent with the public interest and the national economy. By 1970 its goals for the public service were declared 85 percent achieved,[11] a dubious figure and one heatedly debated, for there were those who saw too many inadequately qualified and trained individuals replacing expatriates too hastily for the public good. The most conspicuous example occurred in education: South African teachers were sent home during the early and middle 1970s to make way for a generation of hurriedly trained Swazi graduates, with disastrous consequences for the examination pass rates at the turn of the decade.

Land was likewise both a nationalist and a class issue—albeit less easily identified with a specific interest group. There were actually three issues that concerned land. The first was the Swazi claim that the British had bargained away thousands of square miles of Swazi territory to South Africa as its borders were being delineated during the nineteenth century. When the king accepted the instruments of government in 1968, he rejected those dealing with Swaziland's international boundaries, with the intent of investigating the legal issues and the possibilities for negotiation later.[12]

The second land issue concerned ameliorating the condition of the peasantry on Swazi Nation Land in order to improve productivity and to help counteract the baneful socioeconomic effects of the imbalances in the economy created by postwar capital development. The government implemented an ambitious project, the Rural Development Areas (RDA) scheme, aimed at improving the quality of life and economic prospects of the countryside by targeting specific sectors for development. Its achievements fell consistently short of government aims, which themselves were the subjects of great controversy. But the scheme itself is planned to continue for years to come, and the government maintains high hopes for its eventual success.

The third land question was the most politically charged of all, involving as it did the class interests and deepest aspirations of the growing petite bourgeoisie and at the same time touching the national pride of every Swazi. The problem centered on the festering issue of the European-owned freehold ("title deed") lands, still making up nearly half the country. As the land (much of it owned by South African individuals or companies) came up for sale, speculation was driving up prices so that individual Swazi—even the wealthier ones—were being priced out of the market. There were stories of land rising in price from £8 to £1,000 over the span of a decade.[13] The land in question tended to be the most fertile and best irrigated, which further provoked the already bitter memories of the concessions and of colonial perfidy. The king's attempts to obtain British financing for the repurchase of all lands at the time of independence had been rejected.

In 1972 the government passed the Land Speculation Control Act, designed to halt the sale of land (or immovable property or company equity) to any non-Swazi national unless such a sale was authorized by a control board. It also removed that portion of the increase in land values upon future sale deemed to have been the result of speculation.[14] The act transformed the theretofore serene relations between the country's whites and the new government into a storm of controversy and led to the replacement of the finance minister, Leo Lovell, a liberal ex-South African who had taken up Swazi citizenship. Whites feared the immediate collapse of land values, and over the longer term they viewed the continuation of existing property relations (and the stability they implied) as the sine qua non of Swaziland's future capital development for the ultimate benefit of all. Clearly the government was conscious of its own dilemma, the need to maintain a stable and attractive investment environment on the one hand, while beginning to "restore the land to the people" by at least capping soaring land values on the other. It was well aware of the historical correlation between frustrated land reform movements and political instability, and in the end that consideration prevailed in its implementation of the act. The move proved to be highly popular.

The Land Speculation Control Act's effects since 1972 confirmed neither the worst fears of its opponents nor the highest hopes of its supporters. The control board allowed some land sales to non-Swazis to take place, and Swaziland has continued to attract foreign investment. But the government's claim that by virtue of the act the "people of Swaziland" would once again hold title to "the soil under their feet" has been realized only symbolically, if at all.[15] The real Swazi beneficiaries of the act have been the monarchy (largely through its Tibiyo Taka Ngwane Fund), its clients, and the emerging Swazi elite. Ironically, the commoner remained as landless as ever, outbid by Swazi entrepreneurs in the title deed market and barred by tradition from owning acreage on Swazi Nation Land.

Controversial as it was, the Land Speculation Control Act was in many ways emblematic of what Swaziland had become as an independent and westernized nation. Seen by many as undemocratic, the act had at least been passed in democratic fashion, after open (and heated) debate by a Parliament representative of all social and interest groups. And it had been shepherded through that process by the white successor to Lovell as finance minister, Robert P. Stephens, in the proclaimed interest of the Swazi citizenry.

Yet by the year of the act's passage, the strains that had accompanied independence—new political institutions and alliances, new and accelerated social differentiation, new and pointed popular demands for more of the fruits of independence—had begun to tell. More and more school-leavers combined with disillusioned peasants to accelerate the rural-urban migration, seeking jobs that were relatively less and less available. Unions, although they remained legally sanctioned, were as actively discouraged by the new Swazi government as they had been in the 1960s. The traditional grievance procedure that had been a principal cause of the 1963 strikes, the *induna* (now *ndabazabantu*) system, whereby a company-salaried king's representative mediated union-management disputes, was reinstituted. That "union" was more often than not a plant-level works council; the only government-sanctioned, industry-wide mechanisms were wage boards to establish minimum compensation levels, boards on which government and management together held dominant representation. Resultant worker antagonism, combined with a relative decline in real wages since independence, was an issue easily capitalized upon by the NNLC. Its effectiveness in doing so was seen by the government as the leading cause of the resurgence of labor unrest, which culminated in a strike at the Havelock asbestos mine in early April 1973. "Swaziland," the finance minster declared, was "on the brink of severe industrial strife as a result of the activity of politicians, political parties and outside influences."[16]

Strife there was, but whether it was primarily industrial or largely opposition-inspired was questionable. What was not questioned was that given the galvanic tensions prevailing, the election of 1972 set in motion forces that the government finally deemed stoppable only by the most extreme measures.

It will be recalled that in the 1967 election the NNLC, in spite of winning 20 percent of the popular vote (47 percent in Mphumalanga), had gained no seats in Parliament by virtue of the makeup of the constituencies. In the May 1972 election, Mphumalanga went by a close margin to the NNLC, giving it for the first time three out of the twenty-four seats in the new Parliament. That alone was a rude shock to the king and council, but a demographic analysis of that constituency suggested trends even more ominous. Embracing the major sugar complexes of the country, Mphumalanga contained a heavy percentage of working-class voters drawn from all parts of the country. It also included numbers of smallholder farmers at Vuvulane whose contractual rights with the Vuvulane scheme relieved them of their traditional dependence on the king and chiefs for access to land. The expressed dissatisfaction by those two elements with government policies dominated by the monarchy indicated a threat to the system that carried far beyond Mphumalanga's environs.

The government moved swiftly. Within a week of his election, one of the victorious NNLC candidates, Thomas Ngwenya, was deported to South Africa as an "undesirable" person. The succession of seriocomic events that unfolded over the ensuing months demonstrated how far the forces of traditionalism were prepared to go to ensure their own preservation. Ngwenya appealed, and in September the High Court set aside his deportation order. In October a boycott by Imbokodvo MPs (members of Parliament) prevented Ngwenya's parliamentary swearing-in for lack of a quorum. In November, in an act reminiscent of South Africa's unconstitutional 1955 High Court of Parliament Bill, the Swazi Parliament passed an amendment to the Immigration Act that made the prime minister, not the High Court, the final arbiter in matters of disputed citizenship.[17]

Ngwenya's lawyers' appeals to the High Court on the grounds of the act's unconstitutionality were denied, and they thereupon petitioned the Swaziland Court of Appeal (which, replacing the old British Privy Council as the highest appellate level, seated three leading South African judges). On 29 March 1973 that court ruled that the Immigration Amendment Act was unconstitutional.

Two weeks later, on 12 April 1973, the *ngwenyama* acted. At a public meeting, flanked by cabinet, nobility, and ranking officers of the Swaziland Defence Force (formed only a few days previously), Sobhuza declared the constitution suspended, Parliament dismissed, and all political parties banned. He announced that he would thenceforth rule by decree. The first of those decrees was a six-month measure for sixty-day detention without trial. Shortly thereafter Zwane, Ngwenya, and three other leading NNLC party members were so detained.

Even in a continent where the British legacy of Westminster-style constitutions has been notoriously short-lived, the precipitousness of the king's actions caught most observers off guard. In retrospect, it seems that his dislike of the constitution imposed on him by the departing British had been greatly underestimated. The smashing early successes of the royalist INM had shielded his extreme distaste for the political process it had dominated. As long as Parliament had been filled with royalists, it could be seen as simply a harmless (even beneficial) legislative extension of existing traditional institutions. But the appearance of an official opposition in 1972 replaced that assumption with the specter of a public body first questioning, then seriously eroding, royal authority. That was what was not to be tolerated, the political process itself: "The Constitution [proclaimed the king] has permitted the importation into our country of highly undesirable political practices alien to and incompatible with the way of life in our society, and designed to disrupt and destroy . . . our . . . method of political activity."[18] The result, he went on, had been

Sobhuza II proclaiming the withdrawal of the constitution, 12 April 1973, at the Royal Kraal, Lobamba. Photo from the Swaziland National Archives.

"hostility, bitterness and unrest in our peaceful society." As elaborated by the prime minister and others, the effects of those undesirable political activities, "bordering on the subversive," had been an increasingly unruly NNLC opposition, a trade union movement prone to work stoppages and political activism, and even a judiciary independent to the point of obstructionism.[19] Indeed, it was widely asserted that the formation of the national Defence Force (armed and trained by the South Africans) just prior to the decree stemmed from royal uncertainty over the political reliability of the police.

The suspension of the constitution and related arbitrary measures brought to an end the heady period of social testing and political skirmishing that had characterized postindependence Swaziland. Political opposition was silenced, and union activity was neutralized through the prohibition of meetings of any size.

THE ROYALIST DECADE, 1973–1983

The country's reaction to these events was calm, and the king was notably successful in co-opting or otherwise silencing opposition leaders, but even so, underlying social tensions remained. Periodically they have surfaced in diverse and sometimes seemingly extraneous ways. Labor strikes, often marked by violence, have periodically erupted. A march on the royal residence by railroad workers during a 1975 strike was turned away by police tear gas. Tear gas and mass arrests were again used by police to stop a violent strike by sugar workers at Big Bend in 1978, during which cane fields were set alight. In both cases the issues were wages and the unpopularity of local and Labour Department officials. Dissatisfaction with the grievance system as administered by that department caused work stoppages at the Ezulwini hydroelectric project in 1982.[20]

Most indicative of the social antagonisms that the forced return to traditionalism failed to eliminate were the teacher boycotts and violent student demonstrations in 1977. Again, what was notable was the giving way of the initial grievance, wages, to the venting of hostility toward the underlying system as the stoppages progressed. The 3,000-member Teachers' Association had been struggling for years to improve a wage structure it considered grossly inadequate and to make more responsive a ministerial bureaucracy so inefficient that some teachers were not paid for months on end. Government warnings to the teachers not to carry their unionlike struggle too far were tempered, in 1975, with the establishment of a salaries commission, whose scope of inquiry included teachers' pay and conditions. In 1976 it recommended a pay increase and a job evaluation system to address underlying problems. Teacher anger over the small size of the increase and the slow government response to other recommended reforms led to a mass boycott of classes in October 1977. When the government replied by banning the Teachers' Association and attempting to force the boycotters back to work, students massed in support of the teachers. Over 3,000 strong, they rioted in the two major cities, Mbabane and Manzini, attacked government buildings and property, burned vehicles, and stoned two cabinet officers, including the minister of education. The destruction by all accounts was the most violent since the 1963 labor strikes.

Police, with orders to shoot if necessary (two students were wounded), restored order relatively quickly, and teachers and students gradually returned to their schools. But the events touched off criticism of the king that was without precedent in its scope and bitterness. As Sobhuza addressed the teachers, ordering them back to their classes, scores walked out of the meeting—an unheard-of gesture.[21]

The labor strikes and teacher-student boycotts of the late 1970s were indicative of the frustration with the king's actions in reversing the process of democratization. It was among the working class and the petite bourgeoisie that the dashing of rising expectations was most acutely felt. Strikes and agitation were conspicuous evidence of that, but there were other signs. Social observers saw as another indication of underlying tensions the rise in the incidence of ritual (*muti*) murders in Swaziland beginning in the mid-1970s, a considerable number of them perpetrated by wage earners and school-leavers. Associated with *tinyanga* (practitioners of ritual medicine), *muti* killings had traditionally (though rarely) been prescribed by *tinyanga* in extreme cases to cure illnesses, reverse fortunes in business or in love, or to ensure success in hazardous undertakings. Flesh of the still-living victim (normally the very young or the elderly) was mixed with other elements to concoct a powerful medicine. During the post-1973 decade, ritual murders, a capital offense and an acute embarrassment to Swazi officialdom, reached epidemic proportions. To many, they were indicative of a widespread sense of desperation among those who saw archaic institutions as no defense against the new and bewildering forces confronting them.[22]

The new political order the king had promised when he suspended the constitution was nearly six years in coming. The postdecree tensions felt most keenly by the less advantaged might have been lessened had the replacement of the constitution been as decisive as its suspension had been. Coupled with the decree, the king established a royal constitutional commission. The constitution that would emerge from its deliberations, he said, would be just, fair, and responsive and would take into account Swaziland's unique features and customs—something the previous constitution ("tailored elsewhere") had not done.[23] The commission had been originally to report within a month, but it was not until 1978 that the king announced the constitutional basis for new elections. Selection of MPs for the new Parliament (*libandla*) was to be indirect, with the traditional *tinkhundla* (roughly, community councils, often encompassing several chiefdoms) forwarding slates of candidates to the king for his approval. He could reject whomever he chose and appoint others. Voting in the *tinkhundla* (presided over by the king's representatives) was to be by public, not secret, ballot. Voters would choose an electoral college of 80 from 160 nominees; the college in turn would elect 40 MPs and 10 senators from its own ranks. No political parties were allowed, and the ban on public meetings remained. Parliament's role was limited to debating government proposals and advising the king.[24]

King Sobhuza maintained that the new system reflected the best aspects of both modern Western and traditional Swazi political systems. But observers noted that the new arrangements eliminated the direct responsibility of the government to the people, thus removing a right they had held under the pre-1973 constitution. The power of the monarchy, through the veto, through the power of appointment and dismissal, and through domination of the *tinkhundla* process (rurally based, hence distanced from effective urban-industrial opposition), had never been stronger. Given the realities of its true role, the candor and heat of debate in the new Parliament, at times highly critical of government policy, came as a pleasant surprise to many observers. As openly reported in the independent press, it served to diminish somewhat the popular sense of loss over what had been given and then taken away.

To be sure, what had been withdrawn, the apparatus of Western-style representative government, injured most deeply the sensibilities of those most westernized by background or circumstance. The educated, the urbanized, the industrialized were more apt to judge what had occurred by more rigid, Western standards than were the majority of citizens. It was often forgotten that by contemporary African standards, what appeared in modern Swazi officialdom to be authoritarian or exploitative or even corrupt, were very moderate practices indeed.

Still, the royalist type of government prevailing since 1973 simplified the task of identifying those enjoying real power in Swaziland. Simply stated, they were those men who had held the trust of the king or who had been appointed by him. Parliament after 1973 remained little more than a debating platform.

As late as early 1983, two of Sobhuza's sons by different wives remained cabinet ministers, Prince Gabheni Dlamini, minister for home affairs and for labor, and Prince Nqaba Dlamini, minister for commerce, industry, and mines. The Ministry of Agriculture and Co-operatives was a locus of power in the cabinet by virtue of its able leadership, centering around the minister, A. K. Hlope, the permanent secretary, Arthur Khoza, and the deputy minister, Prince Mahomu Dlamini, who was closely related to the late king. The justice minister, Polycarp Dlamini, a confidant of the king and a holder of high office since the 1950s, survived the king's mass cabinet dismissals in 1979. The prime minister, Prince Mbandla Dlamini, who took office in late 1979, was something of a mysterious figure in the hierarchy of power. The former manager of a sugar estate, he was neither a direct descendant of the king nor a member of the old guard. Yet he gained instant popularity by a number of moves upon attaining office, including the unfreezing of relations with Mozambique, the release of fifteen detainees who had been held for months or years, and the establishment of a commission of inquiry to probe corruption in government and parastatal agencies. But the prime minister subsequently lost status when the king stepped in, in response to intercessions by the old guard, and disbanded the commission. The king's appointment of a traditionalist, Richard V. Dlamini, as foreign minister appeared to weaken the prime minister's position still further.[25]

Great—probably very great—power was held by a number of men who directed or advised the Tibiyo Taka Ngwane Fund, the parastatal development and investment corporation closely held by the monarchy. Simon Sishayi Nxumalo headed it; he was called the second most powerful man in the country while Sobhuza remained alive. He was a former cabinet minister and the king's roving ambassador with the closest ties to him as adviser and confidant ("Sobhuza's eminence grise," said one observer). There were many clashes of interest between Nxumalo and the prime minister after the latter's appointment.[26] The others making up that close circle were all Europeans: Nathan Kirsh, the South African industrialist; Robert D. Friedlander, the attorney for Tibiyo; and Goshe Szokolay, the manager of the Simunye sugar complex. They were said to have amassed between them enormous influence over major decision making in Swaziland.

The king reigned with a firm hand until the last. His popularity was reaffirmed in full measure during the Diamond Jubilee celebrations in September 1981, which by any standard were an impressive national demonstration of love, loyalty, and pride. The ceremony itself was symbolic of his guiding philosophy of a lifetime, the symbiosis of the traditional and the new. The venerable sovereign stepped from his limousine, bare of foot and chest, clad at the waist in leopardskin and adorned with royal feathers, carrying a traditional battle-ax. He walked slowly along a red carpet to inspect the ranks of his modern army in their smart, red-jacketed dress uniforms. Then he came to the field to dance, with his traditional warriors, a part of the same ritual he had performed at his coronation sixty years before.

Sobhuza's lengthy homily touched upon various subjects, all of them symbolic of his many struggles: the absence of trust among nations, the cultural arrogance of the colonizers, the need to strike a balance between time-tested values and modern innovations. He spoke of what he saw as the great challenges to modern Swaziland—with obvious reference to the recent political upheavals he himself had wrought: "The challenge facing you now is to preserve that which is good in your culture, and to adopt what is good in foreign culture regardless of where it comes from. . . . Each nation is trying to identify those things which are good, and to concentrate on the blessings bestowed by God. . . . If it proves necessary," he warned, "a nation will take steps to revive the customs which made [it] whole in the past."[27]

Less than a year later, on 21 August 1982, the king died. Whether the traditional Swazi institutions he so venerated would sustain the kingdom during the trying times that followed his passing remained to be seen. The traditional instruments for the transfer of power were employed once again. They had been in disuse for over eighty years—but in terms of the complexity of the times, the interval seemed measurable only in light-years. Many doubted the capacity of those designated in the traditional manner to deal with the intricacies of the problems confronting them.

The king-designate was a fifteen-year-old, Prince Makhosetive. Until he reached maturity, the country was to be ruled by the queen regent, Dzeliwe, and the sixteen-member *liqoqo*. Dzeliwe was in her mid-fifties, literate in English, and reputed to be strong-willed and intelligent. To assist her in council, Sobhuza before his death had designated an "authorized person," Prince Sozisa, to act in her name. It was said that even the prime minister, Mbandla Dlamini (who was not a member of the *liqoqo*), needed its, or Prince Sozisa's, approval before acting on any matter. Sozisa was in his mid-sixties, and he was reputed to be illiterate and unversed in worldly affairs.[28]

So there was cause for concern. The process of the accrual of power to one individual and his advisers and councillors, as described in these pages, carried with it profound implications for the future. If history was any example, periods of succession following powerful Swazi kings (e.g.,

Sobhuza I and Mswati) were turbulent and dangerous times; and Sobhuza II was arguably the most powerful of them all. The new *ngwenyama* was very young. Much—perhaps too much—would depend on the character of the queen mother.

Beyond the succession, it was to be a time of testing, not only for the monarchy itself, but for all elements of a new society that Sobhuza the youth would scarcely have recognized: an educated elite, ambitious and expectant, desirous of political institutions responsive to modern demands; multinational capital determined to promote its position; an old guard seeking to preserve a status quo the riches of which seemed matched only by the scope of its external encumbrances; and foreign governments and organizations ranging the political spectrum—all with pressing interests to advance. What seemed certain in mid-1983 was that the ensuing months, perhaps years, would witness the playing out of tensions that had been building up for years between the forces of traditionalism and change.

Throughout the uncertainties, however, there prevailed a sense that Swaziland's institutions and its destiny would endure. For one of the kingdom's perennial strengths had been its optimism in the face of any adversity. That spirit had pervaded the Jubilee, the crowds, knowing of Sobhuza's mortal frailty, knowing equally that his spirit was beyond mortality. "He is a perfect king," marveled one participant caught up in that spirit. "This is a land of peace. He'll last, maybe a hundred years."[29] Fortune willing, King Sobhuza's spirit will touch Swaziland for far longer than that.

80

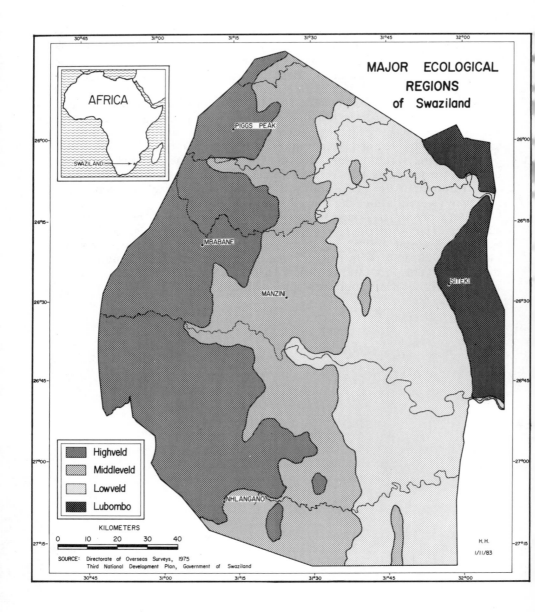

MAJOR ECOLOGICAL
REGIONS
of Swaziland

PIGGS PEAK

MBABANE

MANZINI

SITEKI

NHLANGANO

Highveld
Middleveld
Lowveld
Lubombo

KILOMETERS
0   10   20   30   40

SOURCE: Directorate of Overseas Surveys, 1975
Third National Development Plan, Government of Swaziland

H.H.
1/11/83

4

Geography, Resources, and the Economy

GEOGRAPHY AND CLIMATE

Swaziland is one of the smallest countries in Africa, in terms of both area and population. It is a landlocked kingdom, situated between the Republic of South Africa (to the south, west, and north) and Mozambique (to the east). Its area covers 6,700 sq mi (17,400 sq km), making it a bit smaller than Wales or New Jersey. It is situated mostly between the twenty-sixth and twenty-seventh southern parallels.[1]

Swaziland is compact in shape, the maximum north-south dimension being less than 120 mi (192 km) and that from east to west 90 mi (144 km). The nearest seaport is Maputo, Mozambique, 141 mi (226 km) from Swaziland's capital, Mbabane. It is connected by rail through the border point at Mhlumeni. The new South African bulk port development at Richards Bay, Natal, 231 mi (370 km) from Mbabane, is connected by a new rail line through the Lavumisa border point. Johannesburg, the industrial and commercial center of South Africa, is 244 mi (390 km) from Mbabane. A rail extension is to be built north from Swaziland to link with the South African network at Komatipoort, 111 mi (178 km) from Mbabane, which will incorporate Swaziland entirely into the South African railroad system.

Swaziland's 1983 population was approximately 600,000. The last official census (1976) placed it at 494,534. Both its official population growth rate (2.8 percent per annum) and its infant mortality rate (156 per 1,000 live births) are high, even by African standards.[2] Its population density (82 per sq mi, or 32 per sq km) is, by comparison, about 30 percent below that of Lesotho and 40 percent above that of Zimbabwe.

Although small, Swaziland is a country of great geographical and climatological contrast, a fact that affects deeply all agricultural, resource, and human development of the country. Topographically it is divided into four well-defined regions extending north-south along roughly parallel

81

lines. They are, from west to east, the highveld, the middleveld, the lowveld, and the Lubombo Plateau.

The westernmost belt is the highveld (area 1,900 sq mi [4,900 sq km]), characterized by wild and broken country, especially mountainous in the north and the south. It varies in altitude from 6,000 ft (1,800 m) to 3,500 ft (1,050 m) above sea level. It is underlain by granite, gneiss, and other ancient igneous and metamorphic rocks. The climate is comparatively cool and moist. The capital, Mbabane, is situated in the highveld and has a normal annual rainfall of 53 in (1325 mm) and a temperature range of 73°F (23°C) to 51°F (11°C). The wet season lasts the summer (October through March), and virtually all streams are perennial. Pasturage tends toward short grasses that are "sour" (losing their nutritive value during winter). The highveld is not a good area for intensive growing of subsistence crops. Only about 3 percent of highveld soil is "good, suitable for intensive agriculture, on gentle to moderate slopes." Another 7 percent is considered "fair." The land is inclined to be rocky and boulder-strewn (42 percent by area) and the soils generally deficient (often seriously so) in nutrient elements, so that most subsistence crops need complete fertilization to be grown successfully. The highveld, consequently, does not produce sufficient maize to feed its population.[3]

Fortunately, this same combination of topography and climate has been found over the past forty years to be ideally suited to the growing of coniferous (especially pine) and gum (eucalyptus) trees. In fact, Swaziland's natural and man-made forests—totaling over a quarter million acres (100,000 ha) and constituting one of the major timber and pulp operations in the world—are situated almost exclusively in the highveld. So have been nearly all the major mines—gold, tin, and iron, which are now exhausted, and asbestos, which may last beyond the end of this century.

The middleveld (area 1,700 sq mi [4,600 sq km]), the next belt to the east, is a rolling grassland plateau, with an altitude varying from 3,800 ft (1,140 m) to 1,500 ft (450 m). The climate is subtropical and drier than that of the highveld. Swaziland's second major city, Manzini, is situated in the middleveld and has a normal annual rainfall of 35 in (875 mm). The average temperatures range from 79°F (26°C) to 56°F (13°C). Geologically the middleveld is dominated by granites and gneisses (principally quartzites), which particularly in the upper middleveld have weathered to yield deep soils. Many rivers are perennial, with a few intermittent for several weeks annually. Vegetation consists of tall grasses, not quite as sour as in the highveld in winter, and mixed bush. The middleveld is cattle country, and overgrazing has become a serious problem. Soils tend to be acidic and again not very productive without fertilizer or manure. There are chiefly two soil types, friable red loam and grey loam—the red being the more suitable for agricultural purposes. The three middleveld areas with good soil conditions are the Mlumati basin in the north; the Malkerns-Ezulwini-Mtilane valley region in the center; and the Nhlangano-Dwaleni area in the south.

The middleveld is the area with by far the highest population density, and it is the principal rain-grown cropping region in Swaziland. Maize, mostly for home consumption, covers more than half the ploughed area on Swazi Nation Land and in normal years yields enough to feed the middleveld population. Maize is supplemented by sorghum, vegetables, nuts, fruit, wattle, cotton, and tobacco. Much of the best soil is under irrigation, and the irrigated land is the locus of the greatest agricultural productivity. The greater portion of the irrigated area is title deed (European-owned) land. The largest irrigation scheme is at Malkerns, where pineapples, citrus fruit, and rice are grown. Citrus fruit and bananas are produced in the Mlumati Valley.

The lowveld (2,400 sq mi [6,200 sq km] in area), lying to the east of the middleveld, is by contrast an undulating savanna plain, broken by a few ridges, lying mainly between 1,000 ft (300 m) and 500 ft (150 m) above sea level. The climate is dry and nearly tropical, the average temperature falling between 85°F (29°C) and 60°F (16°C). The vegetation is broad-leaved savanna and tropical bush. Geologically the western lowveld is dominated by Ecca sandstones and shales; underlying the eastern portion are basalt lavas. Coal is found in the Ecca region (near Mpaka). The tall grasses of the lowveld are "sweet"—palatable and nutritious to cattle the year around—but the quality of grazing is totally dependent on rainfall, which is scarcer and less reliable than in the higher elevations, 20 in (500 mm) to 35 in (875mm) per year on the average. The carrying capacity of the lowveld is consequently estimated at 8 acres (3.2 ha) per beast. Overstocking, especially in dry years, is a critical problem.

It is, in fact, water (or the lack of it) on which the viability of the lowveld turns. The soils (mainly clay loams and black clays) are reasonably fertile, especially in the basalt country to the east. But in the lowveld the tributaries of the rivers are ephemeral, and in times of drought the Ngwavuma and the Mbuluzane have been known to go dry. Only the Mbuluzi, the Lusutfu, and the Nkomazi rivers are believed to be completely reliable. The drought hazard (rainfall below 20 in/500 m) for Big Bend is around 56 percent, and since maize needs an annual rainfall of at least 30 in (750 cm) to ensure a successful harvest, it is planted less often than the drought-resistant crops, cotton, sorghum, and groundnuts (peanuts). Even their yields are marginal except in the best of years.

Successful agriculture in the lowveld, then, where a good 80 percent of the soil is arable, is highly dependent on irrigation. The most successful of the irrigated areas are around Balegane and the northern lowveld, Big Bend, and Nsoko. They are, again, largely title deed areas. Sugar is by far the main crop grown, but there are also citrus fruit, cotton, and tobacco. Sweetveld (year-round grazing) ranching on freehold farms possessing water is also highly successful. Since soils tend to be shallow, drainage of irrigated fields poses a particularly challenging engineering problem lest waterlogging and salinity result. Rice, formerly a principal lowveld crop, has for this reason proved more successful in the middleveld.

Road bridge across the Lusutfu River near Siphofaneni in the lowveld. Photo by the author.

Of all the areas of the kingdom, the lowveld has historically posed the greatest rural public health difficulties. Malaria, a massive problem before World War II, has since been largely eradicated, although visitors must still take prophylactic tablets before entering that area for any period of time. Bilharzia (schistosomiasis) remains endemic in the lowveld and in fact is a danger in all parts of the country except the swift-flowing rivers in the mountains of the highveld. Since World War II, because of the reduction of malaria and the growth of the labor-intensive sugar industry, population growth in the lowveld has been dramatic, at times increasing faster, proportionately, than that of the middleveld.

The fourth topographical belt, the Lubombo Plateau, lies to the extreme east, bordering Mozambique. It encompasses 500 sq mi (1,300 sq km), and in altitude, temperature, and rainfall resembles the middleveld. Its west-facing scarp is cut by the gorges of three main rivers, the Lusutfu, Mbuluzi, and Ngwavuma. Geologically it is volcanic (rhyolite), and it is the rockiest of all the regions, with steep slopes that also hinder agriculture. Less than a third of the region is arable, the best areas being concentrated around Siteki and Lomahasha. In the Swazi Nation Land areas, middleveld crops (maize, sorghum, and vegetables) are grown; on the freehold farms ranching is the principal industry.

THE NATURAL RESOURCE BASE:
LAND, WATER, AND MINERALS

Swaziland can be readily seen to possess that combination of topography, soils, and climate that have afforded it a wide range of agricultural and forestry potential, much of which remains to be exploited. There is room for the development of new crops—drought-resistant winter wheat in portions of the lowveld, for instance, and improved pasturage with many times the stock-carrying capacity of natural veld throughout the country.

But a great deal of the land is under use at present, and dramatic increases in agroforestal productivity will require far better use of land already under cultivation, as well as the carefully planned allocation of remaining virgin acreage. It probably will not be physical factors that will hold back future development of abundance and diversification in agriculture; the hurdles can be expected to be largely political.

Current statistics indicate that less than 17 percent of total land area is under cultivation of some sort, including commercial forests, older cleared lands, and fallow (see Table 4.1). Another 30 percent is rocky and steep; still another 10 percent is built up or taken by rivers, canals, roadways, or air facilities. That leaves roughly 43 percent of the land theoretically developable for subsistence and marketable crops. But out of that balance comes grazing lands—already seriously overstocked and eroded in many areas.[4] Clearly a key to greater productivity in the kingdom lies in revolutionizing land and stock management in the more than 70 percent of the country (including rocky terrain) given over to grazing. That will include improving pasture yields and a rigorous program of destocking in many areas, attempts at which have failed repeatedly in the past. As long as the tenure system in the Swazi Nation areas continues to effectively allow free grazing of unlimited numbers of cattle, productivity is unlikely to change substantially. Such a change would involve a fundamental alteration of the underlying political system, which no realistic observer expects to happen under present circumstances.[5]

It seems more feasible, therefore, to improve productivity by better management and more development of the existing loci of cultivation, which amount to only about 9 percent of the "good" and 6 percent of

TABLE 4.1

Land Utilization in Swaziland, 1979-1980 (hectares)

Land-Use Category	Whole Country[a]	Swazi Nation Land	Individual Tenure Farms[b]
i) Cropland	189,363	137,924	51,439
Crops	153,974	108,652	45,322
Fallow	35,389	29,272	6,117
ii) Grazing Land	1,102,054	788,715	313,339
Natural veld	1,034,166	788,715	245,451
Improved	67,888	---	67,888
iii) Commercial Forests	100,618	---	100,618
Pines	72,816	---	72,816
Others	27,802	---	27,802
Other farm land[c]	75,996	4,855[d]	71,141
All other land	221,293	---	221,293
Total land	1,689,324	931,494	757,830

Source: Swaziland Government, Central Statistical Office, Annual Statistical Bulletin, 1980.

[a]Excludes urban areas of approximately 9,300 hectares.
[b]Including Sihoya Swazi Nation Land Sugar Project.
[c]Includes areas of farms, buildings, and services.
[d]Includes Purchase-Land for RDAs and other SNL resettlement schemes.

the "fair" arable land on the most ideal slopes. In addition, much of the foreign-owned freehold land (constituting 13 percent of the total) is not being productively utilized at present and therefore contributes little or nothing to the kingdom's crop production (see Table 4.2).[6]

Swaziland is extremely well endowed with water. Its major rivers generally flow from west to east, traversing all four geographical belts on their passage to the Indian Ocean. There are five major rivers. From the northernmost southward, they are the Mlumati, the Nkomazi, the Mbuluzi, the Lusutfu, and the Ngwavuma.[7] Of the five only two, the Mbuluzi and the Ngwavuma, rise in the kingdom; the Mlumati, Nkomazi, and the Lusutfu all have their sources in South Africa. The Mbuluzi, the Lusutfu, and the Ngwavuma all flow through Mozambique on their way to the ocean. All the kingdom's major rivers are therefore international, a factor that causes concern and that involves negotiation in any water-usage schemes in the region. Of greatest current anxiety are the three main rivers (and their tributaries) that rise in South Africa, all of which are included in South Africa's ongoing dam program. Negotiations with the Republic over water allocation, after years of impasse (complicating present usage and future planning) finally resulted in an agreement of sorts in 1981.

A cattle dip in the middleveld near Luyengo. Cattle are dipped at least once a fortnight to guard against tick-borne diseases of the type that wiped out Swazi herds in the early twentieth century. Photo by the author.

South Africa is free to fill its Pongola Puerta Dam (flooding some Swazi territory), and in return it will conduct a comprehensive investigation of water resources that could be used to the mutual benefit of both countries.[8] Increased afforestation, a voluminous user of water, will also affect the Lusutfu river and its catchment area.

These conditions are not the only ones affecting orderly growth. In Swaziland, a series of broadly riparian water laws, together with generous allocations to nonriparians on the basis of actual use, whether properly efficient or not, have seriously limited the amount of irrigation available for future development—particularly of SNL smallholdings. Laws and economic forces concentrating irrigation systems on title deed land, and patterns of government water apportionment—all dating back to the colonial era—have combined to produce a markedly uneven distribution of water rights that have effectively entrenched the prior rights of European estate owners. One answer to this already serious problem would be to levy water charges on existing users in order to capitalize the system of storage dams necessary to ensure enough water for all, but so far this has not been done.[9]

Still, the potential for irrigated agrarian development on a national scale, if properly legislated and carefully planned, is enormous. By 1980 the total area of irrigated title deed land was roughly 80,000 acres (32,000

TABLE 4.2

Individual Tenure Farms in Swaziland: Number and Total Area By Size, 1979-1980
(hectares)

Size/Class	Number of Farms	Area of Farms	% of Total Area of Farms in Use
Farms in Use			
Below 100 hectares	93	4,595	0.9
100 up to 500 hectares	93	23,508	4.5
500 up to 1,000 hectares	39	28,034	5.3
1,000 up to 2,000 hectares	34	48,868	9.2
2,000 up to 3,000 hectares	17	40,174	7.6
3,000 up to 4,000 hectares	14	48,346	9.1
4,000 up to 5,000 hectares	4	18,710	3.5
5,000 hectares and above	23	317,193	59.9
Total farms in use	317	529,428	100.0
Unused holdings	483	228,402	
Total	800	757,830	

Source: Swaziland Government, Central Statistical Office, Annual Statistical
Bulletin, 1980.

ha); the irrigated SNL area was about 21,500 acres (8,600 ha). Studies
show that the potential nationwide is nearly three times those figures—
300,000 acres (120,000 ha), about 7 percent of the entire kingdom.[10]
    But the sine qua non of this development—which for the sake of
future self-sufficiency in food and employment ought to concentrate on
SNL smallholdings—is the construction of large storage dams. They are
notoriously capital-intensive, and if the unmet goals of the Second National
Development Plan (1973–1977) are any indication, the pressures to divert
storage capacity toward estate-based agriculture at SNL expense appear
irresistible. The Second Development Plan detailed an ambitious scheme
for irrigating SNL land in the Ngomane area between the Mbuluzi and
the Mbuluzane rivers, the largest of the plans focusing on SNL development.
It was postponed and others were modified, all in favor of the development
of irrigated estate-based sugar, notably the completion of the storage dam
at Fairview (Mbuluzi River) supplying the new Simunye complex.[11] Currently
the government is pushing ahead with an ambitious project to develop
the Lusushwana River basin for irrigation and hydroelectric power, involving
the construction of two major storage dams, at Luphohlo and Lozita, with
the first waters to flow from Luphohlo in 1984. It is hoped eventually to
irrigate 74,130 acres (29,650 ha) under this scheme. Feasibility studies are
also being conducted for the irrigation of the lower Lusutfu and Ngwavuma
basins. A debate is currently being waged between competing government
interests over whether the thrust of that effort will be into further estates,

TABLE 4.3

Swazi Nation Land: Area (Hectares) and Production of Major Crops (Metric Tons), 1977-1978, 1978-1979, and 1979-1980

Crop	1977-1978		1978-1979		1979-1980	
	Area	Quantity Produced	Area	Quantity Produced	Area	Quantity Produced
Maize	53,902	96,329	71,145	65,291	71,145	96,735
Groundnuts	2,812	1,589	2,738	1,542	2,740	1,271
Seed cotton	7,013	11,866	17,709	7,069	17,709	11,769
Jugo beans	1,766	2,744	2,581	1,406	2,582	1,406
Sorghum	1,007	538	2,287	1,649	2,288	1,582
Beans	2,116	575	1,138	1,130	1,138	322
Sweet potatoes	550	8,250[a]	560	8,400[a]	560	8,400[a]
Tobacco	582	655	254	286[a]	254	286[a]

Source: Swaziland Government, Central Statistical Office, Annual Statistical Bulletin, 1980.

[a]Estimate.

or alternatively into smallholdings. The outcome of that dispute, which has pitted various government ministries, notably Agriculture, against Tibiyo Taka Ngwane, will indicate much about where future government emphasis will be placed—and where the power lies.[12]

Minerals have been vital to the political economy of Swaziland throughout much of its recorded history. Gold and tin were the first minerals to be produced in any quantity during the nineteenth century, but early hopes for major industries involving those minerals were not realized, and attention shifted to ranching and then cash cropping. The first large-scale investment of British mining capital occurred in 1938, with the development by the firm of Turner and Newall of a chrysolite asbestos mine at Bulembu in the rugged northwest mountains. The resulting company, Havelock Asbestos Mines, was wholly owned by the British until a 40 percent stake was accorded to the Swazi Nation (through Tibiyo Taka Ngwane) in 1972. Terrain and transportation difficulties dictated that an aerial tramway 12.7 mi (20.3 km) long carry the asbestos across the mountains to Barberton, in the Transvaal, where it is shipped by rail to either Maputo or Durban. The mine, which has produced top-quality fiber from high-grade ore, is now running toward the lower grades and will perhaps be exhausted by the end of this decade. Tibiyo has, however, acquired an adjacent concession, which may extend the life of the mine considerably.

Iron ore was a principal export from Swaziland between 1964 and 1980. Rich deposits at Ngwenya in the north-central highveld were intensively mined during that period, the main developer being the South African conglomerate, Anglo-American. Virtually the entire lode was shipped to Japan via a railroad built for the purpose, connecting with the port of Maputo. The project generated controversy and ill-feeling from the beginning, since Anglo-American's concession, reputedly very generous, was granted by the colonial state without any consultation with the king or council. Of its profitability one official later remarked, "Swaziland swapped an iron-ore mine for a railway."[13] Ngwenya, its high- and medium-grade ores exhausted, ceased operations in 1981. There remain quantities of lower-grade ore, there and at other sites in the highveld, but they are unrecoverable under present market conditions.

Anglo-American, through its local subsidiary, Swaziland Collieries Ltd., also operates the country's largest coal mine at Mpaka, in the central lowveld. In 1980 Swaziland exported nearly 140,000 metric tons of coal and consumed an equal amount locally. Depending on international energy markets, coal seems destined to replace iron ore as Swaziland's most important mineral export. Anglo-American's explorations, along with those of British, Swiss, and Japanese consortia, have established deposits in five areas of the lowveld that, once developed, could produce several million tons annually. Much of it is highly valued anthracitic, low-volatile, and low-sulphur coal, said to be the richest form of carbon-based energy other than oil and natural gas. Reserve estimates run as high as 200 million metric tons.

Other known mineral deposits appear to be far less significant to the kingdom's future. There are gold and tin, both being mined on a very modest scale. There are known deposits of kaolin, some base metals, and small quantities of some industrial minerals and ornamental stones. Two diamond deposits were discovered by De Beers in the late 1970s, the principal one at Hlane, but the *ngwenyama* rejected the terms on which the corporation was prepared to exploit them, and they remain in the ground.[14]

AGRICULTURE: THE LEGACY OF THE CONCESSIONS

In practically all of the literature describing Swaziland's economy, particularly its agricultural sector, "economic dualism" dominates the theoretical framework. *Development in Swaziland*, by T.J.D. Fair, G. Murdoch, and H. M. Jones, is the study most given to this dualistic approach, placing Swaziland in a southern African regional core-periphery model, then compartmentalizing the kingdom itself into cores ("primary" and "subsidiary") and periphery. Barclays Bank's *Economic Survey* refers to a "parallelism" in agricultural production. The Swazi government itself speaks of its agricultural sector as "sharply dualistic."[15] The lively debate over the validity of the dual economies theory should surely include the case of Swaziland, but it is sufficient here to identify some aspects of its agricultural sector that do not lend themselves to easy categorization.

At independence, the legacy of the concessions meant that approximately 44 percent of the kingdom was foreign-owned title deed land, and

Distributing maize for drought relief near Maloma in the lowveld, March 1983. The drought, the worst since the 1920s, was particularly acute in the lowveld, where many rivers were dry. Photo by the author.

56 percent was Swazi Nation Land. Presently the SNL portion stands at 60 percent of the kingdom, and on all but a small portion of that exist some 50,000 smallholding farms (homesteads) averaging 7.4 acres (3 ha) in size. These farms are run largely along traditional lines, using family labor and draught animals, and they produce for subsistence. A combination of factors—land tenure policy, customary methods, modern homestead economics, and inadequate marketing facilities—all have contributed to their marginal productivity. About 70 percent of the population reside on SNL, and about half of the people depend directly on traditional agriculture for their livelihood.

The remaining 40 percent of the kingdom[16] is given over to individual tenure farms (ITFs), stemming from the concessions period. They number about 850 and average about 1,977 acres (791 ha). They were owned almost exclusively by foreign individuals and companies at the time of independence, but foreign ownership (partly through the workings of the Land Speculation Control Act of 1972) now amounts to only about 17 percent of the kingdom's land area. In control of the balance, roughly 23 percent of the land, are a number of publicly owned modern farms, run by governmental bodies such as the Ministry of Agriculture, the Prisons Department, and the Defence Force. Others are owned and operated by Tibiyo Taka Ngwane. A few of the modern farms (on no more than 4 or 5 percent of the modern farm area) are on Swazi Nation Land, but utilize up-to-date ITF methods and technology.

Although by no means all the ITFs are highly productive, or even located on the best lands (about 30 percent of them are not), there are a number of large, highly capital-intensive, and technologically advanced and well-managed estates. The greater number of ITFs, although they benefit from the economies of scale and the sophisticated marketing facilities of the others, are more labor- than they are capital-intensive. Whatever these details, there is no question that the ITFs generate high output. They account for upwards of 60 percent of total agricultural production, and their rate of production is growing at nearly 7 percent per year (see Table 4.4).[17]

From what we know about the economics of the "modern" (ITF) and "traditional" (SNL) agricultural sectors, it is difficult to view them as anything but interdependent—and certainly not "sharply dualistic." In the first place, wage levels in the forests, the cane, cotton, and tobacco fields, and the canneries and sawmills are low enough to require those employed to subsist partially on homestead production—for their families if not themselves.[18] Second, the Tibiyo fund, which is held by the king "in trust for the nation," has a heavy and growing equity share in many of the most productive of the ITFs. It is said to pass along these benefits to the people in the form of health care, educational development, support of various institutions, and diverse schemes to achieve national self-sufficiency. In other words, government ideology itself assumes an interdependence between the "modern" and the "traditional" sectors.

Third, there is the question of capital expenditure and the setting of precedents. Accurate, comprehensive figures indicating national priorities do not exist in Swaziland, since there are two separate national revenue and expenditure accounts: the government's, which are open to public scrutiny, and Tibiyo Taka Ngwane's, which are not. But when the government, by its own account, underspends its Second Plan's agricultural development goals by 48 percent (spending a total of E 16.7 million) and diverts water development away from the SNLs to support estate-based irrigation, while during the same period the government and Tibiyo are investing E 26 million in a single ITF (Simunye), it is difficult not to infer an apparent priority, and an interdependence.[19]

It would appear, in short, that in spite of the various assertions of dualism and parallelism of a "modern" and a "traditional" sector, in fact there is in Swaziland a single agricultural economy, in which one sector, embracing most of the land containing the bulk of the population, is helping to subsidize the other.

Government policy to improve SNL quality and productivity remains focused on the Rural Development Area program, which was first implemented prior to independence in 1966. Its inception stemmed from official disquietude over the economic and social effects of rapid postwar capital development and industrialization. While the population remained predominantly (over 90 percent) rural, the dynamism of the commercial sector was by then attracting a disproportionate amount of available capital and

TABLE 4.4

Individual Tenure Farms in Swaziland: Area (Hectares) and Production of Major
Crops (Metric Tons), 1975-1976, 1976-1977, 1977-1978, 1978-1979, and 1979-1980

Crop	Year	Crop Area	Quantity Produced
Sugarcane	1975-1976	19,024	1,867,010
	1976-1977	19,492	1,929,259
	1977-1978	20,239	1,992,274
	1978-1979	21,073	2,242,378
	1979-1980	22,575	2,195,887
Pineapples	1975-1976	1,236	17,937
	1976-1977	1,118	20,842
	1977-1978	(n)	23,355[a]
	1978-1979	(n)	29,869
	1979-1980	1,747	27,553
Cotton	1975-1976	8,910	6,146
	1976-1977	6,894	7,255
	1977-1978	9,253	10,414
	1978-1979	7,353	6,931
	1979-1980	6,464	5,368
Tobacco	1975-1976	252	43
	1976-1977	175	172
	1977-1978	175	172
	1978-1979	342	198
	1979-1980[b]	271	310
Citrus	1975-1976	(n)	74,358
	1976-1977	(n)	64,903
	1977-1978	(n)	61,894
	1978-1979	(n)	62,450
	1979-1980	(n)	57,442
Oranges	1975-1976	(n)	38,492
	1976-1977	(n)	38,244
	1977-1978	(n)	33,983
	1978-1979	(n)	34,913
	1979-1980	(n)	28,713
Grapefruit	1975-1976	(n)	26,651
	1976-1977	(n)	26,659
	1977-1978	(n)	27,911
	1978-1979	(n)	27,537
	1979-1980	(n)	28,727

Source: Swaziland Government, Central Statistical Office, Annual Statistical
Bulletin, 1980.

[a]Estimate.
[b]Freehold and traditional land.

(n) = not available

skilled manpower away from the rural areas. The imbalances and stresses thereby created were becoming increasingly difficult to manage. The government therefore sought means of countering the lure of the urban-industrial areas by improving the quality of life in the countryside. Scientific farming—the use of tractors, improved seeds, fertilizers, and insecticides, all to achieve national self-sufficiency in foodstuffs—was seen as one answer. Another was to increase the number of Swazi homesteads (still fewer than 10 percent of the 40,000 farming families by 1973) involved in commodity (i.e., tobacco and cotton) production.[20]

The RDA scheme, drawing many of its features from the colonial Native Land Settlement scheme of the 1940s and 1950s,[21] designated large tracts of Swazi Nation Land (to number fourteen by the mid-1980s, covering 60 percent of SNL area and involving some 200,000 people) for land development, intensive farming, and the creation of improved communications, marketing, and social services. Those were to include agricultural supply, storage, and marketing depots; pools of mechanical equipment for hire; potable water supplies; "appropriate technology" schools; and health clinics. A crucial feature involved the destocking of Swazi herds by an eventual 15 percent as one of the keys to overall preservation of land resources. It was hoped to double existing RDA income over the span of the Third Development Plan (1978–1983).[22]

The goals of the RDA program, which *in toto* amounted to an ambitious scheme of rural social engineering, consistently fell short of achievement, sometimes seriously. Contrary to the Third Development Plan's goal of self-sufficiency, domestic maize production declined. Studies showed that the typical homestead budget's dependence on cash income from the modern sector increased throughout the plan period, so that in 1981 only 6 percent of the surveyed homesteads were viable on cropping alone. Homestead commodity cropping remained at best a marginal enterprise, and destocking targets were never approached. Finally, in spite of the often admirable achievements of the RDAs, the rate of rural-urban migration rose.[23]

Many observers believed that the key to the RDA scheme's consistent underachievement lay in its basis of traditional land tenure, whereby Swazi Nation Land is retained by the king and distributed in usufruct only through the chiefs. The threat that land usage rights could be withdrawn by those chiefs, however rarely exercised, contributed to a sense of insecurity that inhibited both the development and the productivity of the land. Nor could acreage under that system be used as collateral for credit. Without any fundamental change in land tenure, homesteaders continued to see wage employment supplementing partial subsistence farming as the surest path to advancement.[24] Decline in SNL productivity (minus 1.7 percent during 1978–1981, while that of ITFs grew 6.8 percent over the same span) set officials to questioning the underlying relations of production. "In this context [RDA underproduction]," a recent government report concluded, "the present form of land tenure must be reconsidered, because it does not provide security of investment for the small-scale operator."[25]

In the agribusiness (estate-based farming) sector, it is the marketing aspect rather than productivity that mainly concerns the authorities. World markets for the principal output of those estates, particularly sugar and forest products (Swaziland's two principal foreign exchange earners), have been in recent years exceptionally weak.

Since the 1950s, Swaziland has been recognized as an ideal location for intensive commercial production of sugar. Large-scale cane planting commenced in 1957, and by 1960 two modern processing mills, at Mhlume and Big Bend, had come into operation. In 1980 a third major complex, Simunye, came on line. All of these estates are located in the lowveld and are controlled by British (Commonwealth Development Corporation; Tate & Lyle; Lonrho), Swazi (government; Tibiyo Taka Ngwane), Nigerian, West German, U.S. (Coca Cola), and Japanese (Mitsui) capital. Two additional sugar estates on Swazi Nation Land, at Sihoya and Sivunga, are run by Tibiyo. Sugar is transported by rail to Maputo, thence overseas, principally to Great Britain and other EEC countries, the United States, and Canada.

The development of the Swazi sugar industry has been by any standard impressive. Area under cultivation in 1979, 55,783 acres (22,313 ha), comprised 1.3 percent of the kingdom's land area. The industry is the country's largest employer (60,000 people wholly or partially dependent on it in 1979) and is an important source of government tax revenue through a special sugar levy. With Simunye fully operational, Swaziland's productive capacity has reached approximately 411,000 metric tons per year. Twenty-eight percent of that, 116,000 metric tons, is purchased annually by the EEC at a guaranteed price, Swaziland being a signatory to the Lomé Convention.

But such dramatic development of a single industry carries with it all of the potential dangers inherent in Third World monoculture. Sugar, which contributed 20 percent of the kingdom's foreign earnings in 1972, is expected (depending on the world price) to provide 53 percent by 1983. The world price for sugar has slumped since 1980, leaving the three-quarters of Swaziland's productive capacity that is unprotected by EEC guarantees subject to the erratic fluctuations of the marketplace. "This reliance on a single crop for export and foreign exchange earnings," economic analysts warn, "introduces an element of insecurity into the market."[26]

Forest products are Swaziland's second largest export earner, triple the value of its leading mineral export, asbestos. Commercial timber plantations, started by Peak Timbers in 1947, cover some 237,216 acres (94,886 ha), or 5 percent of the land. Pines and other conifers, grown both for pulp and for sawn timber, take up 73 percent of the forest area. Eucalyptus, mainly for mining timbers, accounts for 25 percent; and wattle, used for tanning, makes up the remaining 2 percent. Nearly all these forests are in the highveld, concentrated around Mhlambanyati, Bhunya, Piggs Peak, Nhlangano, and Gege. In addition, Swazi Nation Land contains another 12,355 acres (4,942 ha) of forest, mostly wattle.[27]

Usutu Pulp Company Ltd. mill and timberland at Bhunya in the highveld. Photo by the author.

Peak Timbers (a subsidiary of Anglo-American) and Usutu Pulp (owned by Courtaulds and CDC) are the two major timber companies operating in Swaziland. Peak Timbers operates two sawmills, exporting principally to South Africa, Zambia, and the Persian Gulf countries. Usutu owns one of the largest commercial forests in the world, with an estimated 55 million trees. It exports kraft pulp to South Africa, Europe, Asia, and South America. In 1981 Courtaulds and CDC announced the sale of Usutu Pulp to Anglo-American for a reported E 110 million, but it was postponed pending negotiations with the Swazi government, which reportedly objected to the sale of such an important resource without its being consulted. It was also said to have demanded for the Tibiyo Fund an equity share in the new ownership arrangement.

Although the world market for forest products was weak during the early 1980s, the prospects for a recovery and for expansion of Swaziland's forest industries were good. Ample land and sufficient water were said to be available, and the prospects for significantly increasing the pulp forest area and timber employment, if the sale to Anglo-American materialized, were high. Development of a wattle bark processing industry also seemed promising.

Swaziland is a significant exporter of a number of other agricultural products.[28] Citrus fruit (mainly grapefruit and oranges) is grown in irrigated fields, most successfully in the lowveld. Swaziland's Lomé Convention

Pineapple field in the Malkerns Valley in the middleveld. The valley, fully irrigated from the Lusutfu River, is one of the richest agricultural areas in the world. Photo by the author.

membership again bolsters export prices to the EEC, and Swaziland also ships quantities to the Middle East. Non-export-grade fruit is processed at the Malkerns cannery or shipped to South Africa. Pineapples provide another significant export, mostly canned or as juice. They are processed by the Nestlé subsidiary, Libby Swaziland, at Malkerns. Pineapples can be grown by dry-land farming methods. Although prices have recently been depressed, the EEC again buys a portion of the crop at the guaranteed price.

Rice, once thought to be a promising export crop, has gradually been deemphasized because of a weak world market and the buildup of salinity in lowveld irrigated fields. Its growth is now concentrated in the Malkerns-Matsapha area in the middleveld, mainly for export to South Africa and for local consumption. By contrast, cotton has become an increasingly important export crop, especially to the Swazi smallholder farmer. It is grown on ITFs as well, but by 1980 over 60 percent of the total crop was being produced by small-scale growers. The crop is exported mainly to South Africa. There are two ginneries, one at Matsapha, the other a new project combining a ginnery and seed oil mill near Big Bend. It is hoped that the cottonseed oil mill will lead to the development of a vegetable oil industry involving sunflowers and groundnuts, and in time to the establishment of a margarine plant and cattle feedlots.

Tobacco is another cash export crop that is being grown with increasing success by Swazi smallholders. As with cotton, government cooperatives provide credit facilities, and technical and marketing assistance to beginning farmers. What is not consumed locally is exported to South Africa. Avocados, bananas, granadillas, mangoes, pecans, and other more or less exotic crops are also grown for export. Beef is exported on a modest scale, shipped frozen to the EEC and canned to Britain, South Africa, and Mozambique. Import and export statistics are found in Tables 4.5 and 4.6.

INDUSTRY AND TOURISM

Swaziland's involvement in agribusiness since World War II has taught it both the benefits and the dangers of involvement in the world economy. Sugar, forestry, and other ventures have brought prosperity, including badly needed employment opportunities, to many segments. But they have also demonstrated the hazards of dependency on foreign market forces.

Swaziland, like many developing countries, has sought to moderate these hazards by diversifying into other industries, mainly light manufacturing, food processing, and tourism. In doing so, it has confronted the dilemma of creating conditions attractive enough to lure foreign investment, while ensuring that it, not foreign capital, maintains control. Few would disagree that Swaziland's efforts to negotiate that narrow line have not been entirely successful. No African countries have.

As outlined in the Third Development Plan, the government's goals for industrial development address both targets to achieve and risks to avoid. They could be the criteria for dozens of developing countries throughout the world. Industries are sought that are labor-intensive and that will contribute to rapid and orderly industrial growth. They are wanted to provide opportunities for the training and advancement of local workers and managers, particularly in less developed areas of the kingdom. Especially desired are those industries that will increase the value of local natural resources by processing them, at least partially, before export. Finally, industries that decrease Swaziland's dependence on imported goods and that increase exports beyond the southern African region are encouraged.[29]

In order to foster such investment, Swaziland has established two parastatal organizations whose aims are to facilitate and subsidize industrial growth. The parent body is the National Industrial Development Corporation of Swaziland (NIDCS). With a 1980 capitalization of approximately E 12.4 million, it promotes development through loans, grants, and capital investments to industries whose initial equity is greater than E 100,000. It provides factories for lease or sale, undertakes feasibility studies, and provides liaison with other government agencies. It was NIDCS that promoted the Big Bend ginnery and cottonseed mill, the manufacture of particle board out of local eucalyptus, and—along with other ventures— a ceramics industry, using kaolin deposits near Nhlangano. These and other projects, if they proceed as planned, will involve a commitment of some E 30 million and employ perhaps 3,000 people away from the concentrated Mbabane-Matsapha corridor.

The Small Enterprises Development Company (SEDCO), a wholly owned subsidiary of NIDCS, aims to foster local undertakings for enterprises

TABLE 4.5

Swaziland Import Statistics, July 1978 to June 1979, and July 1979 to June 1980

Commodity	Value (Emalangeni)	% of Imports
i) Food and Live Animals		
1978-1979	17,782,000	6.0
1979-1980	22,795,000	7.1
ii) Beverages and Tobacco		
1978-1979	6,834,000	2.3
1979-1980	5,445,000	1.7
iii) Crude Materials (Inedible)		
1978-1979	1,199,000	0.4
1979-1980	1,925,000	0.6
iv) Mineral Fuels and Lubricants		
1978-1979	28,779,000	9.7
1979-1980	56,166,000	17.4
v) Animal, Vegetable Oils and Fats		
1978-1979	670,000	0.2
1979-1980	310,000	0.1
vi) Chemicals and Chemical Products		
1978-1979	22,355,000	7.5
1979-1980	25,326,000	7.9
vii) Manufactures by Materials		
1978-1979	25,304,000	8.5
1979-1980	35,525,000	11.0
viii) Machinery and Transport		
1978-1979	65,467,000	22.1
1979-1980	60,381,000	18.7
ix) Miscellaneous Manufactures		
1978-1979	17,740,000	6.0
1979-1980	20,082,000	6.2
x) Commodities Not Classified by Kind		
1978-1979	110,731,000	37.3
1979-1980	94,535,000	29.3
Total	296,861,000	100.0

Source: Barclays Bank, Swaziland: An Economic Survey and Businessman's Guide (Mbabane: Barclays Bank Ltd., 1981).

TABLE 4.6

Swaziland Export Statistics, 1979, 1980, and 1981 (Partial)

Year	Volume (Metric Tons)	Value (Emalangeni)	% of Total Exports
i) Sugar			
1979	223,600	69,136,000	36
1980	300,200	128,445,000	47
1981	327,000[a]	126,000 000[a]	(n)
ii) Woodpulp			
1979	161,000[a]	28,156,000	15
1980	156,000[a]	37,273,000[a]	14
1981	156,000[a]	46,000,000[a]	(n)
iii) Asbestos			
1979	37,200	17,558,000	9
1980	31,400	15,590,000	6
1981	(n)	(n)	(n)
iv) Iron Ore			
1979	956,700	5,265,000	2
1980	514,500	3,691,000	1
1981	(n)	(n)	(n)
v) Fertilizer			
1979	45,000	9,976,000	5
1980	96,800	23,670,000	9
1981	(n)	36,000,000[a]	(n)
vi) Coal			
1979	165,200	2,918,000	1
1980	139,600	2,944,000	1
1981	119,000[a]	3,000,000[a]	(n)
vii) Electron/Equipment			
1979	(n)	3,529,000	(n)
1980	(n)	8,181,000	(n)
1981	(n)	(n)	(n)
viii) Meat and Meat Products			
1979	8,431,000	9,055,000	(n)
1980	5,662,300[a]	9,586,000[a]	(n)
1981	(n)	(n)	(n)
ix) Canned Fruit			
1979	(n)	9,184,000	(n)
1980	(n)	9,365,000	(n)
1981	(n)	(n)	(n)

TABLE 4.6 (continued)

Year	Volume (Metric Tons)	Value (Emalangeni)	% of Total Exports
x) Citrus Fruit			
1979	46,200	9,437,000	(n)
1980	40,000	7,646,000	(n)
1981	(n)	(n)	(n)
xi) Sawn Timber			
1979	72,400	8,787,000	(n)
1980	60,800[a]	9,670,000[a]	(n)
1981	(n)	(n)	(n)
xii) Other Exports			
1979	(n)	22,273,000	(n)
1980	(n)	19,805,000[a]	(n)
1981	(n)	(n)	(n)

Sources: Swaziland Government, Prime Minister's Office, Department of Economic Planning and Statistics, "Economic Survey 1978-1981" (Mbabane, mimeo, 1982); Barclays Bank, Swaziland: An Economic Survey and Businessman's Guide (Mbabane: Barclays Bank Ltd., 1981).

[a]Figure approximate.

(n) = not available

of less than E 100,000 in capitalization. Its aim is to develop locally owned enterprises, emphasizing those industries that will create rural employment and lessen Swaziland's dependence on imported consumer items. It offers technological and business management training, subsidized factory and business accommodation, and low-interest loans for working capital and machinery. It also assists in sales promotion and marketing. As of 1980, SEDCO industrial estates had been sited at the main population centers, and 200 Swazi entrepreneurs had been assisted. Its most conspicuous success was the glass factory at Ngwenya, which produces a variety of hand-blown glass objects from recycled glass.[30]

These efforts and a great deal of independent foreign investment (discussed below) have resulted in the development of a diversified and growing light industrial base in Swaziland. Aside from the agricultural and forest products processing already described, there are plants geared to the manufacture of furniture, candy and beverages, clothing and zippers, chemicals, paper products and printing, cutlery, television sets, light tractors, and a wide range of handicrafts. Many of these industries are located at the country's main industrial site at Matsapha or at Mbabane. Industrial estates are being developed at Ngwenya in the north and Nhlangano in the south, both in the highveld near major transport routes to the Transvaal.

Although Swaziland is surely one of the scenic garden spots of the subcontinent, early postindependence hopes for tourism as a major industry

TABLE 4.7

Swaziland's Gross Domestic Product at Factor Cost, 1978-1981 at 1980 Prices, By
Kind of Economic Activity (in Millions of Emalangeni): All Figures Provisional

Activities	1978	1979	1980	1981	% of 1980 GDP	Compound Growth Rate 1978-81 (%)
ITF farms	49,676	48,737	56,409	59,624		6.8 ⎤
Swazi Nation Land	19,391	15,031	19,295	18,716		(1.7) ⎦ [3.9]
Livestock changes	1,480	2,644	(289)			
Forestry	7,680	7,187	7,837	7,900		
Subtotal	77,627	73,599	83,252	86,240	23.3	2.8
Mining, quarrying (excluding iron ore)	15,382	14,509	14,073	14,384	3.9	(2.2)
Manufacturing	77,728	81,102	88,285	96,810	24.7	7.6
Construction	32,732	19,861	12,913	14,000	3.6	(24.6)
Public administration (central)	41,848	44,131	47,555	50,598	13.3	6.5
Distribution (hotels, restaurants)	32,317	37,255	39,773	42,500	11.1	9.5
Other sectors (*)	78,628	67,992	71,213	75,741	19.9	(1.2)
Total	356,262	338,449	357,064	380,273	99.8	2.2

Source: Swaziland Government, Prime Minister's Office, Department of Economic
Planning and Statistics, "Economic Review 1978-1981" (Mbabane, mimeo, 1982).

(*) Includes transport, banking, insurance, real estate, business services,
personal services, etc.

have not been fully realized. There are no more scenic mountains, waterfalls,
or other natural attractions than are found in the kingdom, and two wildlife
sanctuaries add to its attractiveness. The Holiday Inns group operates four
hotels in the country, but the average length of stay by guests dropped
by 20 percent from the middle to the late 1970s.

The reason apparently lies in the nature of what Swaziland's major
tourist market, the South African vacationer, seems to be seeking along
with scenery—gambling and other domestically forbidden social activities.
Swaziland's surge in tourist popularity (drawing principally from Johannesburg and Durban) began with the building of its gambling casino in
the early 1970s. But with the establishment of similar attractions in the
semi-independent homelands closer to the South African population centers
(notably Bophuthatswana's Sun City, a two-and-one-half hour drive from
Johannesburg), Swaziland's anticipated growth in tourism has not met
initial expectations. A second gambling facility at Nhlangano opened in
1980, and a new hotel and casino are planned for Piggs Peak, which it
is hoped will attract visitors from nearby Kruger National Park, a major
South African tourist attraction.

The danger Swaziland faces in its ambitions to attract foreign development capital are typical of developing countries. Capital seeks to exploit, and as much as possible to control, its theater of investment. Practically speaking, no new nation wishing to secure its place in the modern world can avoid seeking development capital, as aggressively as it can, from wherever it is able. The competition to do so is keen; consequently Swaziland, along with other countries, offers generous incentives to potential investors. The difficulty, of course, is to draw the line between development and exploitation. Whether Swaziland has crossed that line is a matter of controversy.

Swaziland offers generous allowances in the calculation of taxable income for the first few years of operation to investors, in the form of depreciation and investment concessions. They amount, in many cases, to a virtual tax holiday for the first five years and an inviting tax environment for the succeeding five or ten. Initial losses may be carried forward indefinitely as write-offs against future taxes. There is a generous allowance for the repatriation of earnings and dividends within the Rand Monetary Area.

Furthermore, Swaziland makes a point of its low wage structure and absence of unions in its promotional literature. The 1980 NIDCS brochure stated, "Wages in Swaziland are low even when compared with those of other African countries." The Bank Workers' Union, it went on, was the kingdom's "only . . . effective trade union; . . . strikes are rare in Swaziland."[31]

The NIDCS literature also cited as a virtue Swaziland's membership in the Southern African Customs Union (involving South Africa, Swaziland, Lesotho, and Botswana) and its incorporation into the Rand Monetary Area. But neither association is regarded as an unmitigated blessing to the kingdom by economists. The Customs Union, first established in 1910, was renegotiated in 1969. It provides for the tariff-free movement of goods among the four countries and allows for the three smaller nations to collect 2.58 percent of total union customs revenues in accordance with a multiplier-factor formula.

Although Swaziland obtains more than half its total revenue from the Customs Union (55 percent, to amount to an estimated E 90 million in 1982-1983),[32] and is absolved from maintaining a costly customs bureaucracy, whether the customs agreement in its entirety is a net advantage or disadvantage to Swaziland is a matter of some debate. Certainly it has its drawbacks. The kingdom imports 90 percent of its goods from South Africa, all of which enter duty-free. Furthermore, South Africa, although obliged to consult the smaller countries, retains "the right to determine the customs, excise, and sales duty tariffs" and in fact does so to its own interest. In spite of the agreement's provisions for the "free interchange of goods," South Africa has prevented the establishment of industries in the smaller countries that it feared would provide unwanted competition. By simply announcing that it would not purchase their products, South Africa effectively forced the postponement of plans for a fertilizer factory

A casual roadside food market in the lowveld near Maloma. Photo by the author.

in Swaziland and the abandonment of an automobile assembly plant in Lesotho.[33]

Swaziland's incorporation into the Rand Monetary Area pegs the value of the lilangeni to the rand, meaning that effective control over the kingdom's monetary policy is partly in the hands of South Africa. South African devaluation of the rand, for instance, would also devalue the lilangeni, whether or not that suited Swaziland's needs. Thus, although Swaziland's incorporation into South Africa's customs and monetary areas holds many of the advantages that NIDCS proclaims, investors must judge whether the costs to Swaziland's economy—loss of autonomy and creation of dependency—are worth the gains.

But the main concern about Swaziland's economic independence lies with the Swazi authorities themselves. In the early 1980s the Swazi government was all too aware of the spillover effect of South Africa's rapid inflation on its own economy and its inability to do much about it. "So long as Swaziland is a member of the Southern African Customs Union and Rand Monetary Area," it warned, "policy options to limit inflation are severely limited."[34] One has only to recall the degree to which British and South African capital dominates Swaziland's natural resource–based industries. Subordination goes much further. World export of Swaziland's citrus fruit, cotton, and other produce is tied in with South African marketing boards. Swaziland's beer industry is effectively monopolized by South African Breweries through its local subsidiary. Anglo-American, if the Usutu Forest sale is consummated, will control 90 percent of the kingdom's forest products industry, as well as dominating virtually all of its current coal production. Anglo-American also owns 50 percent of Swaziland's meat-processing corporation and a leading automobile franchise.

Swaziland's chemical industry is foreign owned. British (Barclays Bank) and South African (Standard Bank) capital dominate its banking network. South African and U.S. capital operate the kingdom's hotels and casinos. The South African industrial magnate, Nathan Kirsh, through his various enterprises, principally the holding company Swaki, dominates Swaziland's maize importation and milling businesses; owns the lucrative Datsun and Mercedes-Benz franchises; controls the two largest trade, hardware, and agricultural wholesale houses (Metro and Swaziland Whole-sale); owns a timber estate and plastics and medical drugs factories; and is the developer of the country's two largest and most modern shopping plazas.[35]

When one tabulates the extent to which foreign capital—mainly South African, but also British, Swiss, German, Japanese, U.S., and other—has moved into control in Swaziland during the postwar years, it is possible to begin to imagine the amount of national wealth that is being expatriated and the autonomy that has been relinquished. Independence brought many rewards and new dimensions to the lives of the Swazi people, including a sense of control over their own destinies. But economically and monetarily, "independence" for them has become a decidedly relative term.

PARTNERSHIP IN CAPITAL DEVELOPMENT: THE TIBIYO TAKA NGWANE FUND

Tibiyo Taka Ngwane means "the wealth of the Swazi Nation." The organization's origins lie in the independence constitution, which vested control over Swaziland's mineral wealth in the *ngwenyama* in trust for the nation. It will be recalled that the question of whether minerals were to be vested in the king in council or in the parliamentary government energized Swaziland's party politics during the 1960s. It was a central issue dividing Imbokodvo (representing the king's interests) from the NNLC (fostering those of the petite bourgeoisie).

The king's victory resulted in the establishment in 1968 of the Tibiyo Fund (as it has become known, or simply "Tibiyo"), into which all revenues derived from mineral royalties were to be deposited. Tibiyo acquired interests in foreign-owned asbestos, iron ore, coal, and other minerals and then used those revenues to expand its interests into agribusiness, industry, and tourism. It has done this by acquiring shareholdings in a large number of major companies (as examples, 32.5 percent of the Holiday Inns group [hotels and casinos], 40 percent of Swaziland Breweries, and 50 percent of Roberts Construction). It also participates in joint ventures with other investors—for example, the Royal Swazi airline, a bank, and the insurance monopoly, Tibiyo Insurance Brokers. It owns its own newspaper, the *Swazi Observer*.[36]

No one knows how successful these ventures have been, since there is no public accountability of Tibiyo's balance sheet. Not every undertaking has made money: The airline reportedly loses E 3 to E 4 million annually; a sparkling new clothing factory stands idle, a monument to inadequate market research, at Nhlangano; and an ocean shipping line has been a spectacular fiasco.[37] But Tibiyo has accumulated enough capital so that a second fund, Tisuka Taka Ngwane, was spun off from it in 1975 to manage the original mineral royalties, with Tibiyo thenceforward becoming self-financing through its other holdings and ventures.[38]

There is no question that Tibiyo Taka Ngwane brings great benefits to the people of Swaziland. It is, as its own literature states, deeply involved in the development of scientific farming, ranching, and dairying with an aim "to make Swaziland self-sufficient in all its basic food requirements at the earliest possible date." Through its major holdings in natural resource exploitation, it "has acted as a stimulus and catalyst to progress and development within Swaziland." It has supported both education, through high school, university, and overseas study scholarships, and cultural and traditional institutions. Not the least of its accomplishments has been the repurchase of 100,000 acres (40,500 ha) of land from foreign control for Swazi use, both for "national projects" on title deed land and for "Swazi traditional occupation."[39]

Furthermore, it is claimed that it is the Swazi Nation that has real ownership of the fund, and with it the right to know of its activities. Its advertisement in the *Times of Swaziland* states: "Tibiyo is owned by the Swazi Nation. Every Swazi national is an owner in Tibiyo—even those just born today. All Swazis have the right to know about Tibiyo activities—how it works and what it does. As in all national matters, all Swazis have the right to appeal to the king with any query about the activities of Tibiyo."[40]

Yet in fact few Swazi know the details of Tibiyo's operations. Its accounts are kept separate from the public revenue and are not subject to the same public scrutiny the national budget receives in Parliament. The Third National Development Plan does not once mention Tibiyo by name.[41] Its resources are entirely under the control of the *ngwenyama* and its board of trustees, which serves at his pleasure. It is subject to no government taxation. Its revenues do not accrue to the Ministry of Finance, in Mbabane, but to Tibiyo House, at Lozithehlezi, the king's palace. Those revenues, among their many other benefits to the Swazi nation, feed, clothe, and provide medical care for the army.[42]

It appears to many, in short, that the Tibiyo Fund has become the vehicle for the item most conspicuously lacking to the royal house at the time of independence, a secure capital base for the reproduction of the monarchy. Those who adhere to the theory of dual economies would do well to observe closely the workings of the Tibiyo Fund, for, in the words of one recent viewer, "In a dependent, peripheral economy with a limited potential for domestic capital formation, Tibiyo has emerged as the major vehicle for domestic capital accumulation" in Swaziland.[43]

What seems disturbing about all this to many observers is not only the fact of capital accumulation, and the power that goes with it. For in a very real sense much of what the Tibiyo advertisements claim is true. The fund belongs to every Swazi national just as much as the king's cattle herds do. The holding of Tibiyo by the *ngwenyama* in trust for the nation is in the essence of Swazi tradition. What is new, and is of growing concern, is the monarchy's alliance, through Tibiyo, with foreign capital. Those concerned with Africa's future, whatever their nationality or ideology, cannot be heartened by the outcomes of postindependence alliances between local elites and multinational capital elsewhere in the continent, whether they be in Kenya, Nigeria, or Zaire.[44] Even the most impartial viewer knows that capitalism tends to subordinate and often to subvert and that a powerful defense against these dangers is free public inquiry.

There is no questioning Sobhuza's wisdom in guiding his nation, or his shrewdness in buttressing the monarchy, throughout his lifetime. But the king has now departed, and the great question of the moment is where the real power in Tibiyo's alliance with foreign capital lies, now that the succession is under way. It is a question that cannot be answered from the outside. In the eyes of many, it is the question on which Swaziland's future turns.

5

Swaziland's International Relations

IDENTITIES

With the approach of independence in the former British protectorates in the mid-1960s, it was the trend for scholars and international agencies to group Botswana, Lesotho, and Swaziland together as the "BLS Territories." Then they seemed to be the quintessential peripheral states, dependent upon South Africa for their imports, their currencies, employment, even for their food and energy resources and the transport necessary to deliver them. They were, in the view of many, "bantustans" by another name, classic peripheral economics. By the 1980s, however, the three had become very different countries in nearly every important respect.

Certainly few people would talk of Swaziland now as a modern-day "bantustan." To be sure, the threats to its independence, both economic and political, are numerous. But Swaziland, with all its vulnerabilities, is internationally recognized as independent, and it has corresponding options.

Swaziland has diplomatic relations with all of the major Western powers and with many of those Third World nations with Western leanings (as well as some that are not so Western: Guinea, Zambia, Tanzania, and Mozambique, for example). Several countries maintain full-fledged embassies in Mbabane, notably the United States, the United Kingdom, and Israel; others use nonresident ambassadors or high commissioners with credentials to more than one African country. Swaziland has trade agreements with still other nations: among others, Gabon, Ghana, Malawi, Nigeria, and Sweden. Swaziland maintains no formal relations with Moscow, Peking, or Pretoria.[1] It is an independent member of a number of regional and world organizations (the most important are the Organization of African Unity and the United Nations) and is affiliated with others (the European Economic Community [EEC], from which it receives beneficial treatment as a sugar and meat exporter under the Lomé Convention).[2]

TABLE 5.1

Absentee Africans at Successive Censuses

Census	Males	Females	Total
1911	8,400	100	8,500
1921	5,839	151	5,990
1936	9,451	110	9,561
1946	8,254	423	8,677
1956	10,569	1,159	11,728
1966	12,817	6,402	19,219
1976	18,903	6,747	25,650

Sources: Swaziland Government, Report on the 1966 Swaziland Population Census (Mbabane: Central Statistical Office, 1968); Swaziland Government, Report on the 1976 Swaziland Population Census: Volume II, Statistical Tables (Mbabane: Central Statistical Office, 1980).

Swaziland's history and politics have always been profoundly influenced by geographic and economic conditions. They remain so today. Swaziland has for over a century dealt at a disadvantage with foreigners—first as concessionaires, then as colonials, and finally as entrepreneurs—and it is now coping with the consequences of those dealings. This has been so in large part because of what the foreigners found attractive—the kingdom's wealth in natural resources and its strategic location. Politically its rulers have, in compensation for its vulnerabilities (a country small in size and few in numbers defending so coveted a location and so much wealth), sought strength in tradition. To a degree, they found it. Conservatism in land tenure, in resource husbandry, in governance, have accorded a sense of stability that has sustained both ruler and ruled in a world that became more complex and more threatening. It is by no means certain, however, that reliance on custom is any way to meet the new challenges confronting the kingdom.

Many of these challenges are rooted in the past, and they add up to the massive problems of dependency on South Africa's economy and vulnerability to its military power. They are problems the other BLS territories face to differing degrees and, beyond them, ones that affect all states in the subcontinent as far north as the equator. A look at those problems from a regional (especially BLS) point of view will lend some perspective to Swaziland's choice of responses.

First, Swaziland, along with Botswana and Lesotho, has been incorporated into South Africa's migrant labor "catchment area" for the better part of a century (see Tables 5.1 and 5.2). Swaziland's role in that labor market has only recently begun to be investigated,[3] but that system's baneful consequences on Swazi society have a familiar ring: poverty-stricken, fatherless families; illegitimacy and malnutrition; low homestead productivity; and all the other consequences of a nation's exporting a most

TABLE 5.2

People Recruited from Swaziland for Mines in South Africa, 1970-1982

Period	Gold Mines	Platinum Mines	Coal Mines	Total
1970	8,820	215	291	9,326
1971	6,474	180	312	6,966
1972	6,463	438	314	7,215
1973	7,079	780	231	8,090
1974	8,207	1,143	224	9,574
1975	16,272	475	257	17,004
1976	18,652	1,640	451	20,743
1977	13,615	1,302	574	15,491
1978	(n)	(n)	(n)	12,153
1979	(n)	(n)	(n)	11,297
1980	(n)	(n)	(n)	9,367
1981	(n)	(n)	(n)	10,284
1982	(n)	(n)	(n)	12,243

Sources: Swaziland Government, Central Statistical Office, Annual Statistical Bulletin, 1978; TEBA (The Employment Bureau of Africa) Office, Mbabane.

(n) = not available

precious resource—its young men. Swaziland over the years contributed fewer men than the others to the gold mines in absolute numbers, although as a percentage of the total male population its loss was as significant as Botswana's. Neither of them approach Lesotho's dependency, which remains virtually total.[4]

It is a sign of the state of the regional economy that as destructive as the migrant system is, if each of the BLS countries could double the current number of its migrant laborers, it would assuredly do so. Swaziland, which is producing annually 7,000 school-leavers while creating roughly 4,000 new jobs, is on the verge of an unemployment problem, in the late king's words, of "crisis proportions."[5]

Indications are, however, that the migrant flow from the BLS countries will if anything diminish, for both economic and political reasons. The economic factor is twofold. First, as the price of gold rose in the late 1970s—dramatically in 1979–1980—South Africa's mines used part of the capital to mechanize their operations, a venture that had been previously impossible because of the expense of the high technology involved. Since the late 1970s the more modern mines have consequently begun hiring fewer but more highly skilled miners. Pay has increased dramatically, and a bonus system encourages repeated contract renewals for skilled miners, so that gold mining has been a lucrative career for a select group. But that has meant smaller numbers entering the migrant stream.

That labor pool became even smaller with the tumbling of the gold price during the early 1980s, when all gold mines cut back production and employment and the less efficient ones threatened closure. Swaziland, like the other countries, was therefore sending fewer skilled laborers, and hardly more than occasional novices, to the mines during 1982.

Added to this were political factors in South Africa over which Swaziland had equally little control. Beginning in the mid-1970s, South Africa began to reverse its long-standing policy of relying primarily on foreign migrant labor for its mining industry. It did so because of an abrupt and disrupting cancellation of Malawi's supply of miners following a tragic air crash in 1974, and because the mid-1970s (particularly 1977) witnessed the beginnings of violence among certain groups of foreign laborers in the gold mines (in the 1977 instance, Rhodesians). Those and other events[6] coincided with the establishment of the semi-independent homelands beginning in 1976, which produced a more plentiful and predictable supply of more manageable laborers, on which the Chamber of Mines has increasingly relied ever since. The resulting adjustments Swaziland has had to face, although (along with Botswana's) serious, are in no way of the order of magnitude of Lesotho's. That country, whose main source of foreign earnings since independence has been exported labor to South Africa, is in a constantly precarious position, which it must consider in all of its dealings with its neighbor.

Swaziland's membership, along with Botswana and Lesotho, in the Southern African Customs Union has been a second source of concern. Each country sees that relationship as inhibitive of autonomy and restrictive of development. Under the customs agreement (though by no means entirely because of it), trade between these countries and South Africa consists largely of raw materials exports from them to it, and manufactures from it to them—goods that are much more profitable, and duty-free under the agreement. All (Swaziland the least of the three) have thereby built up huge trade deficits with South Africa. Furthermore, some of the major world exports of each (Botswana's beef and minerals; Swaziland's citrus fruit and cotton; Lesotho's wool and mohair) are handled on their way by South Africa's marketing boards and corporations.

Each of the BLS countries is taking various measures to help break this economic grip. Botswana to date has probably been the most successful, and Lesotho most certainly the least, partly because the latter nation is entirely surrounded by South Africa and has no alternative communications routes. South Africa, in fact, continues to hold a virtual monopoly over each country's import and export traffic (90 percent in Swaziland's case), which adds to their dependency, and Swaziland is further enmeshing itself into this network.

The three countries' monetary systems are to varying degrees associated with the Rand Monetary Area and with other foreign banking powers. Both the lilangeni of Swaziland and Lesotho's maluti are pegged directly to the rand. Botswana pulled its pula out of that arrangement in 1976 and, in the face of dire predictions, has seen it consistently outperform the rand. Swaziland and Lesotho continued to suffer all the economic disadvantages of monetary integration. They were not represented on the South African Reserve Bank and thus were unable to influence monetary policies that were likely to affect their economies. The rand's devaluation or the reverse would affect their exports and imports and produce other, often unpredictable consequences. In 1971 these dangers were brought home abruptly to the BLS countries. South Africa, in response to a drop in the gold price on top of some cost increases in its principal imports, tightened up bank credit over the entire monetary area. That slowed down all development programs in the three smaller countries that depended on bank credit. When South Africa simultaneously devalued the rand, the BLS authorities heard about it first through the radio and newspapers.

The arrangement has other disadvantages for Swaziland. Although it is required to deposit a percentage of its reserves in the South African Reserve Bank, it receives interest payments only to the extent that rands circulate in its own economy.[7] Nor has it proved possible, with pegged currencies, for the kingdom to effectively control the outflow of capital to South Africa, its main foreign investor. Continued domination of its banking system by foreign enterprises with heavy commitments in South Africa—the Barclays and Standard groups particularly—does nothing to ease the problem of capital outflow.[8]

OPTIONS

The degree to which both South Africa and the states surrounding it viewed economic ties and dependencies as important was highlighted in 1979 by two events. One was the November 1979 launching of the "Constellation of States" concept by South Africa's Prime Minister P. W. Botha, aimed at providing an ambitious array of regional development cooperation and support programs to be spearheaded by the Republic. Generally it involved a wide range of projects in transportation, communications, water and energy, and agricultural productivity and food supply, which with the substantial support (and leadership) of South Africa was designed to bring about the development and prosperity of all states in the subcontinent. The Botha plan was built around a core of states: South Africa (including the homelands), Namibia, the BLS countries, and Zimbabwe (which Botha at that time anticipated would become a client state under the premiership of at best, Abel Muzorewa, and at worst, Joshua Nkomo).

The second event was the formation, also in 1979, of the Southern African Development Coordination Conference (SADCC), which the Botha initiative was partially an attempt to counter. SADCC was established by states in the region grown increasingly apprehensive about their dependence on South Africa and determined to take measures to reverse it. Besides Swaziland they included Angola, Botswana, Mozambique, Tanzania, Malawi, Lesotho, Zambia, and Zimbabwe. Meeting in Lusaka during April 1980, the conference produced its initial manifesto, the Lusaka Declaration

("Southern Africa: Toward Economic Liberation"), which avowed its commitment to a reduction of dependence on South Africa through individual state intervention and joint activities, such as regional manpower development, industrial and energy coordination, and economic planning. It declared the need to mobilize financial and other resources in pursuance of these goals and to seek international support.

In November 1980 SADCC met again in Maputo in order to formulate programs of action on its three top priorities: independent transportation systems, communications networks, and security of food supplies—all to be free from South African domination. It also attracted pledges of over $650 million in support from some thirty-odd countries and institutions. Envisioned was a multiyear program to refurbish and link together regional rail, road, air, pipeline, harbor, and telecommunications systems (many of them war damaged) in an independent network. Mozambique was the focal point: The transportation systems and trade not only of Swaziland, but of Botswana, Malawi, Zambia, and Zimbabwe are, or could be, oriented toward that country, so the reconstruction and modernization of Mozambique's infrastructure drew nearly 40 percent of SADCC's initial projects.[9] Initially the goals were the repair of the pipeline from Beira to Umtali, to allow importation of petroleum products for Zimbabwe and Botswana; the dredging of the Beira harbor; and the restoration of rail connections from Zambia and Zimbabwe to Beira and Maputo.

Plans to enhance food subsistence and security included increased production, improved storage facilities, joint approaches to food aid and importing, and emergency food transfers between member states. Maize imports from South Africa, which to SADCC countries were upwards of 750,000 metric tons during 1980-1981, were seen clearly as an area of major vulnerability.

SADCC's underlying rationale is that economic dependence limits its members' political options and that regional cooperation can eliminate South African hegemony as both clearinghouse and broker. In July 1982 SADCC heads of state met again in Botswana, where they set up a permanent secretariat headquartered in Gaborone. There is a notable lack of ideological rhetoric involved in SADCC's manifestos and programs, stemming from the remarkably different economic systems among its membership. Four countries follow basically capitalist strategies with varying degrees of state participation and intervention; two are Marxist systems; and three are committed to "transition to socialism" strategies.[10]

Swaziland's role in SADCC affairs has not been without its ambiguities. As a founding member of the organization, it is committed to SADCC goals. It has been assigned, like all members, its own area of responsibility (in its case, manpower development and training facilities). Yet Swaziland's conservatism, and even more its growing economic clientage to South Africa, have led to some questioning of its resolve. Swaziland from the beginning of the deliberations leading to SADCC's formation was seen as one of the countries in the region least firmly committed to economic liberation from South Africa (the others being Lesotho and Malawi).[11]

Swaziland's basic dilemma was highlighted during 1980 by its construction of a rail link south across its border to Richards Bay and to
Durban. Economically the move makes eminently good sense. Richards
Bay when completed will be one of the largest and most modern port
facilities in the world for coal and other bulk resources. It would afford
Swaziland's sugar an alternative to Maputo, which has not recovered from
the exodus of Portuguese technicians in 1975. It would also link all of
Anglo-American's Swazi forestry products holdings with its processing
facilities being built at Richards Bay. Developing coal exports would make
the route all the more attractive.

During 1981 an additional rail link with South Africa was approved,
and it is expected to come into operation by 1984. Known as the northern
rail link, it will run from Komatipoort in the Transvaal through Mhlume
(for sugar) and Mpaka (coal) and connect with the southern route to
Richards Bay. For South Africa the project will reduce the rail distance
and the gradients traversed between the eastern Transvaal and the Natal
ports; for Swaziland it will mean increased revenues and complete integration with South Africa's modern rail infrastructure.

But it will also mean that Swaziland, a charter member of SADCC,
is moving counter to the organization's top priority of forging a transportation network independent of South Africa as a means of reducing
dependency. That South Africa is aware of this politically subversive effect
was confirmed during its assembly debate (the Komatipoort extension
requiring parliamentary approval), which talked of the scheme's helping
to "cement and improve relationships with Swaziland."[12]

Still, ambiguities in commitment by certain SADCC members (Swaziland is not entirely alone in that: Botswana is aiming its own railroad
across occupied Namibia to the Atlantic) detract only in detail from a
basic overall commitment.[13] Certainly South Africa is taking their posture
seriously; but it, too, is faced with ambiguities in shaping its response.
For SADCC, although it is definitely part of the southern African liberation
struggle, is by its very nature passive and benign. It not only eschews
violence: It cannot even be called a boycott. It is, as the Lusaka Declaration
makes clear, a peaceful organization committed to the coordination of
economic programs for regional development.

South Africa has consequently acted very circumspectly against SADCC,
while hardly concealing its dislike for the organization. Pretoria's policy
has been to view SADCC as but one element in an overall threat to its
own regional—hence national—security and therefore to include SADCC
as one of its targets for neutralization, subversion, and destabilization. In
pursuance of this policy, South Africa has made Swaziland a principal
target for co-option—a choice that is to a degree ironic, for Swaziland in
many ways would appear to pose the least of all threats to Pretoria's
designs. But South Africa appears to be enjoying considerable success in
its Swaziland initiative.

Part of South Africa's overall policy in the region has been to selectively
demonstrate the overwhelming economic power that it does possess. To

Zimbabwe, whose 1980 election of the Marxist candidate Robert Mugabe as premier both shocked and frightened South Africa, the lessons have been especially explicit. South Africa canceled for a time a preferential trade agreement, repatriated 20,000 Zimbabweans working in South Africa, and withdrew its locomotives and technicians from Zimbabwe's rail system. It took the latter measure (simultaneously creating a scarcity of diesel fuel) precisely at the time of Zimbabwe's greatest need, the export of its bumper maize harvest in 1981. During the same period, South Africa's campaign to destablilize the Mugabe government through subversion, bombings, and assassinations has prevented the Zimbabwe regime from fully concentrating on an orderly reconstruction of Zimbabwe's economy and infrastructure.

In Mozambique, a South African–trained and –supported insurgency movement, the National Resistance Movement (MNR), some 6,000 strong, has conducted a successful campaign of disruption and sabotage concentrating precisely on those facilities that SADCC looks to for its initial successes—the harbor facilities at Beira and its rail and road links to the interior. A specific target has been the vital Beira-to-Umtali (Zimbabwe) pipeline. South Africa has also severely cut back the flow of migrant labor it has allowed from Mozambique. In early 1981 it showed its muscle, Israeli-style, by conducting a night commando raid against African National Congress installations at Maputo. South Africa's threatening posture and destabilizing actions prompted a summit meeting held at Mbabane in April 1981 involving the BLS countries and Mozambique to discuss regional security and economic solidarity, talks that involved King Sobhuza himself.

South Africa has balanced these actions with more humanitarian measures. There was such crippling drought in the subcontinent during 1982 that only two SADCC countries, Zimbabwe and Malawi, were able to feed themselves. South Africa shipped maize to the others at subsidized prices—three-quarters of the price charged in Zimbabwe—to supplement their depleted harvests. Critics looked on the shipments as a way to promote continued dependence on South Africa as both a food supplier and a critical link in the regional transportation network. At the very least, it was a clear demonstration to SADCC that after three years of existence, its dependence on the dynamism of South Africa's economy was largely undiminished.[14]

It is easy to depict rather bleakly a Swaziland with no options: a country so dominated within and without by South African power and vitality that even reducing that influence appears to be a major undertaking. Yet there remains a wider world that, although Swaziland is barely visible on some strategic maps, sees the kingdom as one element in the search of solutions to the "South African problem." The question is to what degree Swaziland can utilize this position in its quest for a destiny on its own terms.

Swaziland takes some advantage of its strategic situation. Regionally, its relations with Mozambique—which neighbors it but ideologically is a world away—are improving. It has forged diplomatic, trade, transportation (including rail and air) and communications, and water agreements with Maputo. The two governments regularly consult at the ministerial (and often head-of-state) level about concerns over South Africa.

On the world scale, Swaziland's position has also helped it to sharply increase in recent years the amount of aid it receives from foreign countries and organizations. In 1980 that amounted to about $77 million, of which $10 million came from the United States. The EEC, through various agencies, is contributing nearly $20 million in loans and grants toward the Third Development Plan. Other aid, principally from the United Kingdom, the United States, West Germany, the Republic of China (Taiwan), and the World Bank, is directed toward various rural and water development, technical assistance, and educational programs. The United Nations also maintains several rural health and other development programs. Much of the international aid finds its way into various showpiece RDA schemes.

In its function of helping Swaziland achieve self-sufficiency, the degree of success this foreign aid has achieved is a matter of some dispute. It has assisted in a number of worthwhile development projects, but it has not satisfied much of the foreign aid community in Swaziland, which sees too much of it devoted to highly visible but superficial projects while most investment remains concentrated in the export sector, continuing to make profits for the few. Many aid officials view the assistance to the RDA program as investment in a purely technical "fix" of the underlying problem of agricultural productivity whose only real solution is land tenure reform. They see the money spent on the educational system producing ever smaller percentages of qualified graduates. World Bank president Robert McNamara, in a 1980 visit, criticized the government for its planning priorities. And in truth, too much of Swaziland's population remains after fifteen years of independence as one journalist—a bit overdramatically—described it: "Desperately poor, almost beyond a Westerner's ability to fathom. They typically have one set of ragged clothes, patched many times over, eat the same maize meal concoction day in and day out, live in mud-walled huts, often at a great distance from water supplies of dubious safety, and burn firewood because they can't afford kerosene. Eating meat, even catching a bus to town, are major economic undertakings."[15]

CONSTRAINTS

Two issues more than any others highlighted in the early 1980s the cruel dilemma in which Swaziland's regional position placed it. One was over its handling of South African refugees, and the other concerned the kingdom's claims to land.

Swaziland, and indeed each of the BLS countries, has been a logical destination for anyone fleeing South Africa in search of refuge. Swaziland's border (along with those of Botswana and Lesotho) has been repeatedly violated, from well before independence up to the present, by South African authorities seeking to recapture refugees and by their agents bent on assassination, kidnapping, or revenge. In 1963 Dennis Brutus, a South African refugee given asylum by Swaziland, was tricked across the border by a South African agent. In 1982 an ANC official, Petrus Nyahosa, and his wife were killed by a land mine placed beneath his car at Matsapha.[16] Incidents during the intervening years have been numerous.

Swaziland's long-standing vulnerability to such South African behavior is too obvious to warrant much elaboration. Its police force, although British-trained and increasingly competent, is no match in numbers or sophistication for South Africa's establishment. Its army guards mainly against internal dissent. Geopolitically Swaziland since 1975 has stood, Belgium-like, between Marxist Mozambique and Nationalist South Africa, trying as best it could to at least regulate the behavior, if not the flow, of agents and arms moving in both directions. Its successes to date may best be described as occasional.

The refugee problem became acute after mid-1976, when, as the result of the Soweto violence and the South African government's response, Swaziland (along with the other BLS countries) was inundated with young refugees seeking asylum. Both the ANC and its rival, the Pan-Africanist Congress (PAC), exiled from South Africa since 1960, quickly responded to this opportunity by recruiting the youths and sending them for guerrilla training to Angola, Algeria, and elsewhere. Refugee camps in Swaziland soon came to be centers of rivalry between the ANC and the PAC, and the contention turned violent in 1978. Some fifty PAC members were rounded up at that point and deported to Mozambique and beyond, and thenceforward the ANC has dominated the anti–South African scene in Swaziland. Dozens of refugees still cross into Swaziland each month, some in transit for military training, others remaining to start a new life, hoping one day to return to their homeland in peace.

In fact, Swaziland's official involvement with the ANC extends back to the year of its founding in South Africa in 1912. The queen regent, Gwamile, was an early supporter, providing the funds, it is said, for the press that printed its first newspaper, *Abantu la Bafo*. King Sobhuza was a subscribing member of the Congress for many years. But the ANC first established a notable presence in Swaziland only in the early 1960s, following the Sharpeville massacre, which resulted in the banning of the organization and the flight of many of its members abroad. Skeletal directorates were established in each of the BLS territories then, but it was further afield (in Dar es Salaam and Lusaka) that the ANC established its major presence as the 1960s wore on and newly independent Tanzania and Zambia committed themselves to the liberation struggle to the south. Swaziland became a major theater for the ANC only in the mid-1970s, after Mozambique had achieved its independence and following the Soweto eruptions.

The presence and activities of the ANC in Swaziland are seldom officially discussed, although they are obviously subjects of considerable government sensitivity. Swaziland's official position is that it will not allow any organization to use its territory as a springboard for attacks against South Africa, but the degree to which it has been able to control the course of events (e.g., the transit of men and munitions westward from Mozambique) has not been clear.

The South African government has applied mounting pressure on the Swazi authorities to restrict ANC activities and has repeatedly demonstrated its willingness to assist in the process, whether or not Swaziland wished that aid. In June 1980, following the successful ANC sabotaging of the SASOL II facility (South Africa's second—and showpiece—petroleum-from-coal plant) in the Transvaal, believed to have been initiated in Swaziland, South African agents bombed two suspected ANC houses in Manzini, killing two (one an exiled South African student) and damaging forty structures. In February 1981 another South African exile, Dayan Pillay, was kidnapped from St. Joseph's School near Manzini and taken to South Africa for interrogation. He was returned only after his abductors were arrested and charged by the Swazi authorities, leading to the exchange of the detainees. South African pressure on Swaziland continued to escalate. In February 1982 the ANC director of operations in Swaziland was reassigned to Dar es Salaam and was not replaced. In December 1982, after South Africa's raid on the ANC in Lesotho's capital, Swazi authorities rounded up forty-odd ANC members in the country and placed them in detention at the Mawelawela camp, near Luyengo.

The issue of the ANC's presence points up the precariousness of the positions of the independent countries on South Africa's periphery. They have, as Swaziland's prime minister, Mbandla Dlamini, articulated from the UN General Assembly rostrum in 1980, "unswerving [commitments to] the principles of non-racial democracy, non-alignment and complete respect for human dignity, justice and peaceful coexistence with all nations."[17] They are, as such, committed to the struggle for human rights and equality in South Africa. But they are also aware of Pretoria's determination to defend its society from what it terms "terrorist attacks" and "sabotage" from any quarter, even if that be from across the borders of sovereign neighboring countries. That it can do so at will is unquestioned.

South Africa has for thirty-five years felt an affinity for Israel's willful sense of self-reliance, stemming from their mutual feelings of isolation and their mistrust of the United Nations. Pretoria has been an admirer and close imitator of Israeli military strategy and tactics. These have included destabilizing and other clandestine activities of various sorts. They have also involved swift and decisive military strikes across borders to destroy hostile forces or installations, irrespective of world opinion. Angola, Mozambique, Zimbabwe, and Lesotho have thus far been the notable targets of those activities, but South Africa's ability to pursue its aims in any direction is not lost on Swaziland. It would be a foolhardy government that failed to take those realities into consideration in shaping its policies.

The land issue concerned the proposed transfer of the South African "homeland" for its Swazi, KaNgwane, to Swaziland. KaNgwane is an irregularly shaped crescent of territory, 56 miles (90 km) long and between 3 and 12 miles (5 and 19 km) wide, which is sandwiched between Swaziland's western and northern borders with South Africa. It contains upwards of 250,000 people, nearly half of whom have been settled there— more or less forcibly—by the South African government since the mid-1970s. It includes no productive farmland to speak of. It used to be gold country: The place names (Joe's Luck, Revolver Creek) still echo the romance of those days; but the names and the romance are all that are left of the minerals. Outside of some undeveloped coal deposits, it is, in the words of one journalist, "an economic wasteland."[18]

Land of opportunity or not, KaNgwane was, to the late king, Swazi territory. It was part of the realm over which Swazi kings had once ruled, signed away to Pretoria by the British in a nineteenth-century border agreement, but by rights, in the Swazi view, theirs. There were those who believed that KaNgwane's reincorporation would have supremely satisfied the dying monarch as the concluding achievement of his reign. The South African government in June 1982 announced that it was going to do just that.

A second parcel of territory, over which the Swazi claim was far more tenuous, was also to be transferred. That was the Ngwavuma region in the southeast, running from the Swazi border to the Indian Ocean. Ngwavuma would give Swaziland access to the sea and a potential harbor at Kosi Bay. But Ngwavuma was part of KwaZulu, the homeland of the Zulu, the largest (and some say the most militant) ethnic group in South Africa. Ngwavuma's inhabitants, mainly Tsonga, had paid tribute to the Zulu back to the days of Shaka. The Swazi had never held control over the area and, until a decade or so ago, had never thought to make such a claim. The Zulu leader and chief minister, Gatsha Buthelezi, was adamant in his defense of Zulu sovereignty. Ngwavuma was inseparable from South Africa; its handing over was the "provocative and dangerous" act of an Afrikaner government "gone politically berserk." Its transfer would make "bloodshed inevitable."[19] "Sovereignty" was a word with powerful meaning to Buthelezi and his followers; he—alone among homeland leaders—had consistently refused Pretoria's offer of "independence" for KwaZulu on grounds of its inseparability from South Africa.

As for KaNgwane itself, it was by no means certain that its population wanted to be incorporated into Swaziland, although both the *ngwenyama* and the South Africans claimed that it did. The KaNgwane Legislative Assembly, before the South Africans dissolved it, had voted overwhelmingly against incorporation. A petition by Swazi chiefs in the homeland had also protested the plan. "We have no wish," asserted KaNgwane's chief minister, Nganani Mabuza, "to be part of a medieval monarchy that rules by decree. We are South Africans and we want to stay in South Africa and fight for a democratic future here." His calls for a referendum in KaNgwane fell on deaf ears in both South Africa and Swaziland.[20]

The implications of the KaNgwane affair went far beyond the lands involved. South Africa's seeming eagerness to cede a foreign land claim,

which it had never done before, seemed prompted by its desire to grant
"independence" to yet another of its homelands and in the bargain gain
something it had long coveted—international recognition of a key element
in its apartheid policy. For in the bargain Swaziland would be agreeing
to the denationalizing of all South African citizens of Swazi origin, many
of whom had never set foot in the kingdom. There were, by some estimates,
nearly 800,000 of them. There were another 135,000 non-Swazis involved,
in Ngwavuma. There was no public discussion of how Swaziland's already
strained economy would cope with even that portion of those numbers
who were actual residents of KaNgwane, who, along with the land involved,
appeared to add nothing to Swaziland's economic potential but increased
dependence on migrant labor to South Africa.

Pretoria appeared to be gaining other benefits from the bargain, not
the least of which was the drawing of Swaziland into its regional security
network. South Africa had constructed an extensive road system throughout
KaNgwane, which its military units had regularly patrolled in search of
infiltrators from the Swazi border into the eastern Transvaal, a major ANC
route from Mozambique. It was widely assumed that those patrols would
be allowed to continue, and perhaps be extended, as part of the incorporation
agreement. The cession of Ngwavuma would have created yet another
buffer by obligating the Swazis to guard the integrity of that strip, which
had become a principal infiltration route from Mozambique into Natal.

Finally, the KaNgwane scheme appeared to commit Swaziland to a
position that ran counter to much that its fellow members of SADCC and
the OAU stood for. Its incorporation would facilitate the extension of the
northern rail link from Komatipoort, thereby reducing South Africa's own
dependence on the port of Maputo. By thus further enmeshing itself in
South Africa's transportation network, Swaziland was arguably offering
itself up as the evening star of Botha's Constellation.

The OAU had historically opposed any action that served to bolster
apartheid or to deny full rights to South Africa's blacks. Furthermore, it
had long since declared its opposition to the alteration of any international
boundaries, including those drawn by the southern Africa's European
colonizers. At the very least, any border alterations had to be endorsed
by the ANC, which was the OAU's spokesman on South Africa. Swaziland,
in risking the opposition of those three organizations over KaNgwane,
seemed to be taking on a lot.

By the end of 1982 two events seemed to have placed the whole
affair in suspension, at least for the moment. The first was the king's
death. It raised the question of subsequent Swazi policy on KaNgwane,
since the issue had been such a personal one with him. The caretakers
reaffirmed Swaziland's commitment to transfer, but it was not clear how
much support remained, or how strong the opposition, widespread within
the government bureaucracy, would prove to be.

More important, in September 1982 the South African Appeal Court
blocked the transfer of Ngwavuma on the grounds that the KwaZulu

government had not been consulted. By year's end Pretoria had rescinded the transfer proclamation, restored the KaNgwane assembly and sovereignty over the land to it, and agreed to pay all of its legal costs. It appeared that at the very least a generous time interval would pass before the issue was raised again.[21]

The entire KaNgwane affair once again reminded the world—as if it needed reminding—of how forcefully South Africa's will could turn the region. It was a sign of Pretoria's determination to press forward with the business of depriving 21 million of its citizens of their birthright and of its powers to co-opt its neighbors and to subvert its enemies in their attempts to organize against it. Whatever else may come of the affair, the exposure of those realities was something that the next generation of Swazi leadership, among all the region's statesmen and strategists concerned with South Africa, would have to take into account for years to come.

6

The Pressures of Modernity

LESSONS OF THE PAST

There is a history behind each of Swaziland's important traditions—traditions that have set the nation's trajectory, for better or worse, through the obstacles that have faced it down through the years.

Land, and issues concerning it, dominate all of Swaziland's history. Central to the consolidation of Dlamini power in the nineteenth century was the royal line's successful solution to the problems of how to defend the land and how to control its tenure. When southern Swaziland proved untenable against the Ndwandwe, Sobhuza I moved his people north to a region more defensible. His successor, Mswati, created a military establishment capable not only of defending and expanding Swazi lands, but of securing Dlamini legitimacy over them as well. This was done both militarily and ritually, from the strategic garrisoning of the army countrywide, to the ceremonial (*Incwala*) consolidation of royal powers over rainfall and crop abundance. The imposition of a system of surplus extraction of a principal product of the land, cattle, was thereby facilitated, ensuring Dlamini mastery over the crucial early stages of class formation.

Land transfer and concessioning have been questions tracing through Swazi history from the earliest days. The most important transactions have involved Europeans, and most of them have resulted in net losses to the Swazi. Modern-day observers mystified by the degree of passion aroused among Swazi on both sides of the KaNgwane issue in the early 1980s would do well to remember that. Swazi tradition has it that the nineteenth-century delineations of its borders in all four compass directions were heavily at their expense. There are so many claims and counterclaims (many of them undocumented) that the truth of the matter will probably never be known, but one thing is certain. The establishment of Swaziland's borders in the north and west (with the Transvaal), the south (Natal), and the east (Mozambique) was done by European commissions and sanctioned by imperialist governments during the heyday of late nineteenth-century colonialism. Disputes were invariably settled in favor of the South Africans and the Portuguese. It was well known, for instance, that in Mswati's day

122

Swazi man combining in his dress the traditional—knobkerrie and leather *lijobo* over waistcloth—and the modern—shirt and coat. Photo by the author.

the Swazi had laid claim to large expanses of territory that a century ago became by border adjustment portions of the Transvaal districts of Ly-denburg, Middelburg, Barberton, and Carolina.[1]

With regard to the concessions, Mswati himself had initiated the process of Swaziland's dissolution. It had been a matter of strategy and of statecraft. Early in his reign the major external threat had been from Zulu attack, so Mswati had ceded lands in the south (some of which he did not own) to the Boers and the Wesleyan missionaries. The idea in part had been to create a buffer of allies along the invasion route. As the years passed and the Boers gradually supplanted the Zulu as the power to be dealt with,[2] Mswati began during the 1860s to grant rights to a number of British settlers to occupy portions of his western territories, adjoining the Transvaal. Many of those concessions were subsequently sold to Pretoria.

How great a role strategic and diplomatic considerations played in Mbandzeni's concessioning debacle we will probably never know, but surely they were minimal. The cessions themselves, and the use the colonial state made of them to take away the land, associated forever in the Swazi consciousness the subjects of land rights and European deviousness. To many modern-day Swazi, particularly the young and educated, the designs of the South African government in ceding KaNgwane appear to be more of the same. They perceive a white government once again mobilizing land policy to achieve European aims at the expense of African interests. From the early nineteenth century to the latter twentieth, the strategy of land transfer has deeply affected the character of Swazi history, and it seems destined to continue to do so.

Inextricably linked with all this has been Swaziland's historic domination by foreign elements. Predecessors of the Pretoria government that has orchestrated the KaNgwane affair have been dabbling in Swazi politics for well over a century. A Boer, Coenraad Vermaak, became the first concessionaire in 1860. Four hundred Boers attended—some say dominated—the installation of Mbandzeni in 1875, and Swaziland thenceforward became host to large numbers of Boer concessionaires and investors. The influx of foreign settlers, British and Boer, that followed the concessions set Swaziland's history apart from those of the countries traditionally regarded as its sister states, Botswana and Lesotho, whose physical domination by foreign elements has been a relatively recent phenomenon. Swaziland's history over the past century or so has been much more reminiscent of Zimbabwe's; and like that country, modern-day Swaziland has sought ways to accommodate to the realities of continued settler dominance while maintaining control over its own destiny. That quest is bound to continue, and its increasing complexities will test the skills and character of future generations of leadership.

Swaziland's dealings with the South Africans and other foreigners would be eased if its relations with its neighbors to the east and south were in better repair. But, as with the Transvaalers, Swazi relations with the Mozambicans and the Zulu have a historical continuity. Those relations have been largely negative. Toward the sea, Swaziland first intervened (unsuccessfully) in Gaza politics in Mswati's day. Subsequently, Swazi relations with the Shangaan also reflected long-standing enmity. The Shangaan resented what they perceived to be excessive Swazi cordiality to the Portuguese colonials, particularly throughout the war of independence in the 1970s. Swazis remember the substantial influx of cheap Shangaan labor from the 1920s until the 1960s, which created tensions not only over jobs but also, on a more fundamental level, over women. Enmity with the Zulu, tracing back to the days of Sobhuza I and Shaka, is sure to be inflamed for years to come by the Ngwavuma affair of the early 1980s, although happily it seems to have been settled as a problem for the moment. There was an important lesson to be learned from all of that: the degree of success South Africa achieved by using parcels of land as dragon's teeth to sow between African nations. They must find better ways to deal with that tactic. Gatsha Buthelezi's shrewd use of South African law stopped the Ngwavuma transfer in 1982, but history tells us that Pretoria can simply change the law. All of this can only complicate the struggle for reducing dependence and achieving human rights in southern Africa.

BURDENS OF THE PRESENT

If historical forces surrounding foreign land dealings and ethnic relations exhibit a certain constancy, so too do many of the domestic problems besetting modern-day Swaziland. They are often complex and interrelated; and even to outsiders unaware of the traditional forces that helped generate them, the challenges they present often appear to defy solution. Indeed, change, to be meaningful, would require Swazi confrontation with some time-honored and deeply held traditions. It would also involve (figuratively and literally) the goring of some people's oxen.

A fundamental challenge is the productivity of the land. Swaziland, a surplus producer throughout most of the nineteenth century, has been a more or less chronic grain importer throughout the twentieth. There were years earlier in this century when Swaziland approached (even achieved) self-sufficiency, but the increase in grain dependency on South Africa during recent decades has been dramatic. Swazi imports, which averaged 3,000 metric tons per year during the 1950s, rose to an annual average of 28,000 metric tons during the 1970s. During that decade more than E 1 million was spent each year on maize imports. Recent studies have shown that at least one-half of all Swazi households are deficit producers of maize.[3]

Governments, both colonial and independent, have repeatedly intervened in the production and the marketing of maize in Swaziland in attempts to reverse this trend. Market price manipulation, subsidy and other incentive schemes, storage and marketing programs, and RDA projects have all produced consistently disappointing results. The causes for the failures are more easily identified than they are changed.

Land tenure appears to most qualified observers to be a root problem. Ownership of land in any society, under whatever economic system, is a primal motivating force. Its emotive power, if measurable, would surely lie behind sex and hunger, but not by much. Humanity's attempts to socialize the means of production in the countryside, under a spectrum of political ideologies, have historically been failures. The world in the latter twentieth century has watched the two socialist giants, the Soviet Union and China, backing away from land policies the scope of whose disasters no natural phenomena could begin to account for, while the Americas and Australia fed them. History suggests that there is a very strong correlation between freehold tenure of the land and its productivity.

In Swaziland the land is held by the king in trust for the nation. It is distributed, in usufruct, through the chiefs, many of whom have the reputation of regarding improvements to the land as threats to their authority over it. Grazing is free, and cattle are the universally recognized store of wealth. Under those circumstances, the economic incentive that any prudent farmer of whatever background would follow would be to invest in cattle to a greater extent than, say, fertilizer or hybrid seed. That is, in part, what has happened to Swaziland, where the cattle-to-land ratio is the highest in all of Africa.

The prospects for real change in the land tenure system under current circumstances are dim, for such change would have to involve the upheaval of political institutions that appear to be becoming more entrenched rather than less so. In one innovative land scheme of less than 3,000 acres (1,215 ha), Vuvulane, can be seen the kernel of the issue. Vuvulane farmers work their smallholdings either in title deed or as holders of twenty-year leases. The scheme's productivity has been phenomenal. But the smallholders, removed from their obligations to the traditional land tenure system for their livelihoods, formed a core of opposition to the king prior to the suspension of the constitution of 1973. Tibiyo has now purchased a half interest in Vuvulane, and there is speculation as to the disposition of the leaseholds as they come up for renewal.

Two points should be emphasized. First, Swaziland is by no means unique in its problems with productivity; it is a continentwide dilemma. Yields have declined in country after country since independence (15 percent for Africa as a whole during the 1970s), and few nations today are self-sustaining. Even countries like Kenya, where capitalist agriculture prevails, have become grain importers. The World Bank's mid-1982 report on the developing countries singled out Africa as the continent most desperately requiring new measures to increase agricultural output.

Second, it is too simple to assume that a shift to freehold tenure of smallholdings would in itself produce surplus yields in Swaziland. Other incentives need to be involved: Grain productivity is but one aspect of a comprehensive economic planning problem facing the country. For there is no dual economy in Swaziland. Farmers do not grow enough to feed themselves because it makes more sense under prevailing conditions to grow a cash crop, or to earn a wage, which will not only purchase the balance of food requirements but will also provide for other family necessities more easily than growing a surplus for sale would. That is one reason why growing unemployment is becoming such a pressing social problem in Swaziland. What is needed is an effective government response to the fact that there is a single economy in the kingdom and that maize self-sufficiency is a matter not for production and marketing planning only, but also for a comprehensive price policy involving not just those areas, but modern-sector wages, employment, and cash crops as well.

This is a fact that some sections of the government are coming to realize. The Ministry of Agriculture and Co-operatives in its 1980 report on maize production and marketing concluded:

> Attempts to approach the maize self-sufficiency objective through price incentives and investments in marketing infrastructures have failed because they have not adequately recognized the linkage between the industrial and agricultural sectors of the economy. No amount of marketing infrastructure investment will result in more maize for sale unless and until the growing of maize for sale provides a return on effort that compares favourably with cash cropping and wage employment opportunities.[4]

A second area of modern-day concern, also tracing its history back through this century, involves ensuring that foreign capital investment works to the net benefit of the Swazi citizenry. As with agricultural productivity, this issue is hardly confined to Swaziland. The government is faced, as are all developing countries, with the problem of creating an investment climate (including the labor market) sufficiently attractive to lure foreign capital without being exploitative. That can be a murky distinction. The Simunye sugar complex, two-thirds owned jointly by the government and Tibiyo, opted against intensive wage employment in favor of high mechanization in the interest of being competitive in the world market. Yet official government policy is to attract capital "with special emphasis on labour-intensive industries."[5]

In this regard, the very closeness with which the Tibiyo Taka Ngwane Fund continues to be held and operated makes it the object of increasing concern among those wishing to see Swaziland control capital penetration rather than being controlled by it. By Third World standards Swaziland is notably free from corruption, but it does exist, and there is widespread concern over the degree of influence foreign interests have managed to leverage over the Tibiyo and Tisuka funds. A commission of inquiry established by the prime minister in 1981 to look into corruption was abolished by the king, but that same year a trial concerning embezzlement from the Tisuka Fund was held. A prominent witness, Zonke Khumalo (the former deputy prime minister), was asked the whereabouts of a sum of E 79,000 that was unaccounted for. "Mice," he replied, "ate it." He was repeating a widely used Swazi euphemism for theft.[6] The issue of Swazi corruption was one aspect of the problem. But the question in the minds of many was whether the real danger to Swaziland's future did not lie just across its borders in the form of similarly disposed creatures of somewhat larger dimensions.

A problem less apparent but in the long run perhaps the most serious of all lay in the field of education. As rich in natural resources as Swaziland is, its most precious asset remains human. It was clear in the early 1980s that Swaziland was not nurturing that asset well. Given the axiom that an educated citizenry is the key to any country's destiny, the kingdom's O-level examination pass rate of 27 percent in 1982 (by contrast, the pass rate of just over 50 percent in Soweto, Johannesburg's black municipality, was considered shocking) did not augur well for Swaziland's future. Concern over the rate sparked a number of newspaper editorials and a lively debate in Parliament. Commentary focused on the low prestige of the teaching profession, stemming in part from poor-quality training and low pay, and on the need for reform in the Ministry of Education. How rapidly the conditions could be reversed was unclear, but the citizenry's sensitivity to the value of education as the accepted means to upward mobility and equality of opportunity[7] offered hope that they would be accorded much higher government priority than in the past.

SWAZILAND IN A WIDER WORLD

The spirit of conservatism that characterizes the domestic problems of Swaziland is an equally dominant element in its world view. King Sobhuza, who in all matters saw traditionalism as a source of strength, viewed moderation as the surest national response to the demands of a complex and threatening world. It was a posture that, on balance, had served the king and the nation well in the past, and it was one Swaziland was seeking to adhere to in the early 1980s.

But the middle course is going to be increasingly difficult to follow in the rapidly changing circumstances and the hardening of positions in contemporary southern Africa. There is serious question in the minds of many whether Swaziland, or any nation in the region, can pursue such a direction for much longer.

Swaziland is caught between two worlds. Geographically it lies interposed between the two conflicting forces of South Africa and Mozambique. It is dependent on both for its continuing prosperity. Through Mozambique Swaziland ships much of its resources to world markets. To South Africa it is tied by both customs and monetary agreements, and to the Republic it sells much of its produce and some of its labor. The bulk of foreign capital invested in Swaziland is South African. The kingdom's options are consequently limited, and with each rand of Johannesburg capital invested in its economy, its room for maneuver is further reduced.

Swaziland in response has sought the middle road. Since the 1960s it has accepted exiled nationalist groups from South Africa, but it has limited their freedom of action, and it finally expelled what was then the more radical of them, the PAC. It treats the ANC gingerly these days, allowing the organization a presence—taking pains to reassure its OAU neighbors that it continues to do so—but denying it a sanctuary for attacks launched on South Africa. For the Republic has made that a deadly game. In late 1982 South Africa's naked threat to reprise the Maputo and Maseru massacres anywhere in the region had its effects on Swaziland, where the Soweto generation of ANC leadership was clapped into concentration camps in the countryside.

The strategy Swaziland has pursued in all of its dealings with South Africa has been filled with ambiguities. On the one hand, it continues to seek South African investments and to export its labor and products there. It has taken steps to expand its communications links (notably rail) with the Republic. It continues its customs, marketing, and monetary arrangements with Pretoria. And, of course, it covets KaNgwane. All of these measures strengthen its dependency on South Africa.

At the same time, Swaziland is an active member in those regional and international bodies that are committed to the overthrow of minority rule in South Africa and to the reduction of peripheral state dependence upon it. The OAU, of which Swaziland is a member, eschews border readjustments as a cardinal precept, just as it opposes any action that furthers the aims of apartheid. Swaziland's participation in the KaNgwane affair runs counter to both principles. Indeed, that entire affair, even if it is now dormant for the moment, has been exceedingly costly for Swaziland's foreign relations. For a quarter of a million people and some lands of great nostalgic but questionable practical value, Swaziland showed itself willing to enter still further into Pretoria's web of dependencies, to lend itself to the establishment of a South African *cordon sanitaire* along its eastern border, and (most likely) to leash in the ANC in the bargain. The kingdom, in other words, was prepared to become the evening star in Botha's Constellation. In that context, it seemingly mattered little any longer whether the KaNgwane deal was consummated or not.

That, in the early 1980s, was Swaziland's dilemma. Rich, beautiful, and productive, the kingdom found itself as part of a community of people, a region, and a world that no longer would allow it the luxury of remaining neutral. And far to the north in 1983 a tragic drama was being played out involving another once rich, beautiful, and productive country that also seemed to be in the wrong place. Surely the Swazi government observed the dismemberment of Lebanon with more than abstract interest and recalled South Africa's fascination with Israeli strategy and tactics— in this case their dealing with a neutral country harboring an irrepressible nationalist movement. To Swaziland, the options open appeared to be narrowing to the nightmarish choice between clienthood as a "homeland" or becoming, like Mozambique, constantly vulnerable to a variety of military threats.

Finally, underlying all uncertainties remained the immediate problems of the succession. Monarchists took heart from the workings of a traditional system that had produced such a wise and crafty king over eighty years previously; and in truth the selection of Sobhuza had been inspired. But others were not so sure. The 1980s seemed to have produced no Gwamile to negotiate the rocks and shoals of foreign intrigues during another prolonged minority. The formidable nature of the challenges, both domestic and foreign, seemed to them to call for mature, experienced, and disciplined leadership soon after the death of the great king. But for the mechanisms by which that could be accomplished there appeared to be no basis in tradition.

Indeed, the course of events over the first months of 1983 underlined the pitfalls of the Swazi method of succession. The names of the new ruler, Makhosetive, and his mother, Latwala, were circulated in the foreign press but remained mysteriously unannounced to the Swazi people (speculation was that his official naming would come only after his schooling was completed).[8] In the absence of decisive central authority, the power struggle between the modernists, led by Prime Minister Prince Mbandla Dlamini, and the traditionalists, notably his archrival, Justice Minister Polycarp Dlamini, along with Richard V. Dlamini, Sishayi Nxumalo, and Abednigo K. Hlope, burst into the open. The prime minister's attempts to send the justice minister safely off as ambassador to Washington, and to face down his *liqoqo*-centered opposition by arresting two of its members for sedition were both reversed by the queen mother. In late March, Dzeliwe removed Prince Mbandla as prime minister and replaced him with a traditionalist, Prince Bhekimpi Dlamini. Reflecting the tensions of these events, the deposed prime minister then fled to South Africa for safety. The replacing of Mbandla, who had threatened to revive the corruption commission and who had opposed the KaNgwane deal, with Bhekimpi, who favored it, had all the trappings of a victorious palace coup by the traditionalists. Most importantly, it signified the emergence of the once-anonymous advisory *liqoqo* as the new locus of effective power (it was called the "Supreme Council of State" in the press) in post-Sobhuza Swaziland. Its members were now highly visible, sworn in by the chief justice, and salaried, while the cabinet appeared relegated to little more than the implementer of *liqoqo*-generated policies.[9] In August 1983 the *liqoqo* cast off all pretence surrounding its true intentions by dismissing queen mother Dzeliwe in a palace coup over the issue of the naming of candidates for the October parliamentary election. It did so by the expedient of officially designating, at long last, Prince Makhosetive as the next *ngwenyama*, which made his mother, Ntombe Latwala, automatically the new queen regent during the remainder of his minority.[10] The year 1993, when the young king would accede to the throne at age twenty-one, appeared farther away than ever.

These uncertainties were made all the more worrisome by questions surrounding the subtle shifting of authority that seemed to be taking place in the kingdom as time went by. The parastatal organizations established in the 1960s and 1970s to manage natural resources in trust for the people had by the 1980s grown exceedingly wealthy and powerful, but there was doubt as to the degree to which the original trustees remained in control.

Believers in the deleterious forces of neocolonialism in the Third World feared that command of the parastatals, and hence of a massive capital base, was passing from those who had created them. For if one accepts the argument in this volume that Swaziland has been in many ways a classic example of the effects of colonial underdevelopment and the creation of dependency, the temptation to compare what was happening there in the 1980s with what Colin Leys found had befallen underdeveloped Kenya in the 1960s is strong.

Leys concluded that in Kenya the British colonial administration prior to independence had fostered the formation of local strata and classes with an interest in sustaining colonial economic relationships after they were gone. These "comprador elements" (in Chinese terminology) subsequently acquired a large measure of political power and utilized it to maintain the patterns of trade and industrial dependency that had existed before independence. The comprador government, having acquired a stake in the status quo, attracted new capital from abroad on generous terms, entering into a number of joint ventures and suppressing the power of those trade unions whose leadership it was unable to co-opt. Thus, he wrote, a "new process of social and political integration takes place between domestic interests and foreign capital, at various levels . . . progressively articulat[ing] the periphery with the centre, and strengthen[ing] the position of the 'comprador' regimes."

The result in Kenya was a continuation of the structure of exploitation and domination established by colonial rule at the hands of an "auxiliary bourgeoisie" tightly linked to foreign capital. For the mass of the people the consequence was a consolidation of their subjection to the power of capital, which had been initiated with the onset of colonialism. "For the vast majority of the population," Leys concluded, postindependence underdevelopment via the comprador "meant a continuing prospect of hard, unproductive labour mainly for the benefit of others, accompanied by growing inequality, insecurity, social inferiority and the virtually complete absence of political rights."[11]

Many would dispute the emphatic nature of Leys's conclusions about Kenya, and few observers would relate them either in scope or extent to the Swaziland of the early 1980s. Political rights in Swaziland are far from absent, for example; and it is South African, not British, capital that poses the potentially most subversive threat. But the workings of neocolonialism in Kenya, whereby the transition from colonialism to independence effectively transferred political power "to a regime based on the support of social classes linked very closely to the foreign interests which were formerly represented by the colonial state,"[12] bears close attention by the leadership of any Third World country seeking the substance of independence, including Swaziland. The maintenance of true independence is essential for Swaziland, not only for the welfare of its citizenry, but also for the assurance of its national destiny in an increasingly troubled and violent corner of the world.

King Sobhuza II's historic achievement was to preserve Swazi control over his kingdom's destiny during supremely trying times. It falls to a new generation of leadership to ensure the continuity of that control in the even more treacherous era that is just beginning.

Notes

INTRODUCTION

1. The Swazi lilangeni (pl. emalangeni, symbol "E") equaled roughly $1.44 during 1977. In early 1983 it was worth $.95. Hereafter, monetary figures will be in emalangeni. GDP figures are from International Bank for Reconstruction and Development, *1978 World Bank Atlas* (Washington, D.C.: World Bank, 1978).

2. International Labour Office, *Reducing Dependence: A Strategy for Productive Employment and Development in Swaziland* (Addis Ababa: International Labour Office, Jobs and Skills Programme for Africa, 1977), pp. 3–4.

3. Quoted in Shula Marks and Stanley Trapido, "Lord Milner and the South African State," *History Workshop Journal* 8 (1979):52–53.

4. Ibid., p. 52.

CHAPTER 1. HISTORY OF THE SWAZI KINGDOM TO 1963

1. The best single source for the early history of Swaziland is Philip L. Bonner, "The Rise, Consolidation, and Disintegration of Dlamini Power in Swaziland Between 1820 and 1889. A Study in the Relationship Between Foreign Affairs and Internal Political Development" (Ph.D. dissertation, University of London, 1977), to be published by Cambridge University Press. Other important sources include J.S.M. Matsebula, *A History of Swaziland* (London: Longman, 1972); Hilda Kuper, *An African Aristocracy: Rank Among the Swazi* (London: Oxford University Press, 1947); and Lord Hailey, *Native Administration in the British African Territories. Part V, The High Commission Territories: Basutoland, the Bechuanaland Protectorate, and Swaziland* (London: H.M.S.O., 1953).

2. Now known as Old Lobamba, to distinguish it from the present royal residence at Lobamba, which was established many years later.

3. When Shaka, fearing the birth of a male successor, murdered one of the girls, whom he had impregnated, Sobhuza apparently did nothing.

4. After Sobhuza's death, in 1840, Dingane, fleeing the aftermath of his defeat by the Boers and his subsequent deposition, sought refuge in southern Swaziland and was murdered there by a local chief.

5. Philip L. Bonner, "Classes, the Mode of Production and the State in Pre-Colonial Swaziland," in Shula Marks and Anthony Atmore (eds.), *Economy and Society in Pre-Industrial South Africa* (London: Longman, 1980), p. 88.

133

6. Kuper, *African Aristocracy*, pp. 15, 233.

7. Hilda Kuper, *The Swazi* (London: International African Institute, 1952), p. 4, reckons that by the end of Mswati's reign, demographically the Swazi nation was roughly 70 percent Nguni, 25 percent Sotho, and less than 5 percent Tsonga.

8. Thandile was the renowned queen mother known to the Swazi as Lazidze.

9. J. D. Omer-Cooper, *The Zulu Aftermath* (Evanston, Ill.: Northwestern University Press, 1966), pp. 27–28, 50–52, attributes the Swazi adoption of the age-regiment system to their contact with Zulu forces. But it seems reasonable to assume that such close ties as the Swazi had with the Ndwandwe, who also employed the system, made the latter the agents of transfer.

10. Bonner, "Classes," p. 89.

11. Ibid., pp. 89–95; Kuper, *African Aristocracy*, pp. 15, 17–18, 148–153.

12. Omer-Cooper, *Zulu Aftermath*, p. 53.

13. Bonner, "Dlamini Power," p. 363.

14. The guarantor was Sir Garnet Wolseley, administrator of the Transvaal. Matsebula, *History of Swaziland*, pp. 56–61. See also Hailey, *Native Administration*, p. 361; Monica Wilson and Leonard Thompson (eds.), *The Oxford History of South Africa. Volume II: South Africa 1870–1966* (London: Oxford University Press, 1971), pp. 275–276.

15. Kuper, *African Aristocracy*, pp. 24–25.

16. Mbandzeni told visitors before his death that in granting concessions on such a wide scale he had been inspired by the example of the Transvaal government. Hailey, *Native Administration*, p. 362.

17. Allister Miller, "Swaziland in the 80's," Miller Papers, MS Mil 1.08.1 (Ms 577a), Killie Campbell Library, Durban. For Offy Shepstone's career see Bonner, "Dlamini Power," pp. 363–367, 385–417.

18. Johathan S. Crush, "Settler Estate Production, Monopoly Control, and the Imperial Response: The Case of the Swaziland Corporation Ltd.," *African Economic History*, Vol. 8 (Fall 1979):185–186; Johathan S. Crush, "The Colonial Division of Space: The Significance of the Swaziland Land Partition," *International Journal of African Historical Studies* 13, 1 (1980):73–74.

19. Kuper, *African Aristocracy*, pp. 25–26; Martin J. Fransman, "The State and Development of Swaziland, 1960–1977" (Ph.D. dissertation, University of Sussex, 1978), pp. 46–47; Hailey, *Native Administration*, p. 362.

20. One thus revalidated was the Unallotted Lands Concession, which controlled farming and grazing lands comprising about one-sixth of the total land area south of the Nkomazi (formerly Komati) River, in return for an annual rental of £50.

21. Jeff Guy, "The Destruction and Reconstruction of Zulu Society," in Shula Marks and Richard Rathbone (eds.), *Industrialisation and Social Change in South Africa: African Class Formation, Culture, and Consciousness, 1870–1930* (London: Longman 1982), pp. 167–194; Judy Kimble, "Labour Migration in Basutoland, c. 1870–1885," in ibid., pp. 119–141.

22. Shula Marks and Richard Rathbone, "Introduction," in Marks and Rathbone, *Industrialisation and Social Change*, p. 12.

23. Shula Marks and Stanley Trapido, "Lord Milner and the South African State," in Philip Bonner (ed.), *Working Papers in Southern African Studies, Volume 2* (Johannesburg: Ravan Press, 1981), p. 53. Milner's official title was British high commissioner for South Africa and governor of the Cape and Transvaal.

24. The Swaziland Concessions Partition Proclamation of 1907.

25. Crush, "Colonial Division of Space," p. 75.

26. Swaziland has traditionally been grouped with the other two former "BLS territories," Botswana and Lesotho, but the historical parallels in this century between settler-dominated Swaziland and preindependence Zimbabwe (Rhodesia), also settler dominated, are even more striking.

27. Two other men figuring prominently in this period were David Forbes, a miner and rancher, and John Thorburn, a trader, who was also Miller's father-in-law. Miller had been secretary of the White Committee (1887–1890), and as Mbandzeni's adviser (replacing his rival, Shepstone) during the king's last days, had been the architect of much of the most flagrant concessioneering of that frenzied period.

28. Miller to D. O. Malcolm (secretary to Lord Selborne), 21 December 1906, MS Mil 1.08.16 (Ms 429).

29. Miller to Swaziland Corporation, 25 January 1907, MS Mil 1.08.3 (Ms 298B).

30. Cited in Crush, "Colonial Division of Space," p. 81.

31. Ibid., p. 78.

32. Great Britain, *Financial and Economic Situation of Swaziland. Report of the Commission Appointed by the Secretary of State for Dominion Affairs, January 1932* (London: H.M.S.O., 1932), Cmd. 4114. The overstocking continues. Today Swaziland has the largest cattle-to-land ratio in the whole of Africa. Barclays Bank, *Swaziland: An Economic Survey and Businessman's Guide* (Mbabane: Barclays Bank Ltd., 1981), p. 14.

33. As indicated in part by studies demonstrating pediatric malnutrition concentrated in the most underdeveloped Native Areas.

34. The secretary of state, Lord Elgin, misrepresented the true predicament of the Swazi in rejecting the deputation's claims. Given the addition of the Crown Lands, he said, "It is not too much to say that half the lands in Swaziland will be in their occupation." But excepting the sale of one tract in 1914, no Crown Land found its way into any but settler hands until the 1940s. Elgin to the deputation, 10 October 1907, J 45/07, Swaziland National Archives.

35. Figures indicating the amounts thus collected, and the extent of the lands they in turn purchased, are not to be found in the Swaziland National Archives, although they possibly survive in the royal archives at the king's palace, Lozitha, which are restricted. Such figures would help to illuminate the question of motivation, which intrigues scholars studying the efforts of traditional rulers and elites to maintain their control over the relations of production as their societies are subjected to the forces of capital penetration. Close to Swaziland, Patrick Harries ("Kinship, Ideology and the Nature of Pre-Colonial Labour Migration," in Marks and Rathbone, *Industrialisation and Social Change*, pp. 142–166) finds a similar labor tax levied by certain Mozambican chiefs amounting to "direct extortion of a part of the workers' wages" (p. 152). Articles by Guy and Kimble, cited in note 21 above, examine the Zulu and Basotho cases. See also Kevin Shillington, "The Impact of the Diamond Discoveries in the Kimberley Hinterland: Class Formation, Colonialism and Resistance Among the Tlhaping or Griqualand West in the 1870s," in Marks and Rathbone, *Industrialisation and Social Change*, pp. 99–118.

36. From 1916, £1 10s. per male (£1 15s. after 1920), plus 10s. for each wife after the first, to a maximum of £4 10s. per annum. Added to this was a dog tax of 5s. per animal. All state taxation was payable in cash, creating the necessity of wage employment. It would appear that the Swaziland example is similar to what Guy has concluded about the purposes and effects of the Zulu hut tax: It was "a tax on the potential productive capacity of the homestead, the assumption being

that the more wives and the more children within the control of a homestead-head, the greater the wealth of the homestead." "As each year passed," he has found, "so more homesteads lost their self-sufficiency as productive units under the supervisory control of the homestead-head." Guy, "Destruction and Reconstruction of Zulu Society," pp. 175, 189. In Swaziland, the added dog levy further taxed productivity by diminishing ready access to cheap protein, dogs being used for hunting and for cattle and smallstock herding.

37. Ronald Hyam, *The Failure of South African Expansion 1908–1948* (New York: Africana Publishing Corporation, 1972), p. 18.

38. Ibid., pp. 17, 19–20. The schedule, ironically, included a provision for "native land to be inalienable."

39. 1919, quoted in ibid., p. 93.

40. By the 1920s the Boers had taken to referring to themselves as Afrikaners.

41. Hyam, *Failure of South African Expansion*, p. 120.

42. Ibid., pp. 121–124.

43. Great Britain, *Reports of the Transvaal Labour Commission, Minutes of Proceedings and Evidence* (London: H.M.S.O., 1904), Cd. 1897, pp. 100–107; Fransman, "State and Development," pp. 65–69. Contemporary estimates of the absent ranged as high as 65 percent of the male working population. The figure from the 1936 census, which would exclude clandestine migrants, was 9,561, or 24 percent of the male working population.

44. Guy, "Destruction and Reconstruction of Zulu Society," pp. 173–190.

45. Hailey, *Native Administration*, p. 383.

46. Quoted in Hyam, *Failure of South African Expansion*, pp. 117–118, 120. "Whipsnade" in this context means "zoological specimen," Whipsnade being the name of the experimental zoo located outside London.

47. Hailey, *Native Administration*, p. 381.

48. Kuper, *African Aristocracy*, p. 31.

49. Secretary for Swaziland affairs (Governor's Office, Johannesburg) to secretary to the Law Department (with enclosures), 13 August 1906, J 134/06; telegram from high commissioner to secretary of state (with enclosures), 15 December 1906, J 195/06, Swaziland National Archives. During this and other disputes, the government intimidated the queen regent by such acts as openly intercepting her mail and barring her foreign advisers from entering the country or otherwise menacing them.

50. Queen regent to resident commissioner, Zombodze kraal, 26 September 1906, J 134/06, Swaziland National Archives.

51. See, for instance, files S 7 A, J 152-205/06, J 13/07, RCS 506/14, 708/14, 801/14, 100/15, 126/15, 346/17, 281/18, 47/15/883 [1919], and 202/20, Swaziland National Archives. King Sobhuza carried on these practices throughout his reign, and there are indications that some monies went toward the settling of some personal accounts that he had trouble managing during his early years on the throne. An exasperated colonial government intervened periodically, notably in 1926, when the king requested its assistance in the form of a 5s. surtax to help straighten out the royal accounts following his litigation against Allister Miller. The *ngwenyama* could not, however, explain the whereabouts of the £5 per head levy previously collected for that purpose (totaling, by some government estimates, £100,000). King Sobhuza did at that point render a personal accounting of the royal debts (including a lawyer's fee in the Miller affair of £11,000), and the government thereupon collected the 5s. tax. The administration forbade any further Swazi levies, but the exactions never entirely stopped—although they were carried

on thereafter under much closer government scrutiny. Other forms of royal surplus extraction, such as court fines and cattle payments on important occasions, were never monitored. See File 1836 [1926–1927], Swaziland National Archives; Kuper, *African Aristocracy*, p. 31; Hilda Kuper, *Sobhuza II: Ngwenyama and King of Swaziland* (London: Duckworth, 1978), pp. 232–238.

52. Seme, a Zulu educated in Natal and trained in Britain and the United States, played a central role in Swazi affairs, first as protégé of Gwamile and subsequently as adviser to Sobhuza. Seme was also a founder of the African National Congress, of which Sobhuza was a dues-paying member throughout most of his adult life.

53. Hyam, *Failure of South African Expansion*, pp. 98, 149, 161–162. It is notable, in light of the KaNgwane affair in 1982 (see Chapter 5 of this book), that Sobhuza was already in the mid-1930s raising its return to Swazi sovereignty as a central diplomatic issue.

54. Multinational corporations that control Swaziland's sugar and citrus industries include Lonrho, Tate & Lyle, Coca Cola, and Mitsui (sugar); and Libby, a subsidiary of Nestlé (pineapple and citrus fruit).

55. Many of Swaziland's manufacturing, distribution, and service industries are controlled by Kirsh Industries, a South African conglomerate. The tourism industry is dominated by the Holiday Inns group (South African and U.S. capital), which operates four hotels and two casinos.

56. Hyam, *Failure of South African Expansion*, p. 178.

57. Hailey, *Native Administration*, pp. 388–393.

CHAPTER 2. THE SOCIOCULTURAL SYSTEM

1. Hilda Kuper, *An African Aristocracy: Rank Among the Swazi* (London: Oxford University Press, 1947, reprinted 1980). An abbreviated version is Hilda Kuper, *The Swazi* (D. Forde, ed., *Ethnographic Survey of Africa, Part I*) (London: International African Institute, 1952). See also the following: Hilda Kuper, *The Uniform of Colour: A Study of White-Black Relationships in Swaziland* (Johannesburg: Witwatersrand University Press, 1947); Hilda Kuper, *The Swazi: A South African Kingdom* (New York: Holt, Rinehart and Winston, 1963); Brian A. Marwick, *The Swazi: An Ethnographic Account of the Natives of the Swaziland Protectorate* (Cambridge: Cambridge University Press, 1940); Sonya M. Jones, *A Study of Swazi Nutrition: Report of the Swaziland Nutrition Survey 1961–62 for the Swaziland Administration* (Durban: Institute for Social Research, University of Natal, 1963); J. F. Holleman (ed.), *Experiment in Swaziland. Report of the Swaziland Sample Survey 1960 by the Institute of Social Research, University of Natal for the Swaziland Administration* (Cape Town: Oxford University Press, 1964); T. O. Beidelman, "Swazi Royal Ritual," *Africa* 36, 4 (1966):373–405; and Fion de Vletter, *The Swazi Rural Homestead* (Kwaluseni: Social Science Research Unit, University of Swaziland, 1983). Two novels depict Swazi life (in somewhat romanticized fashion): Allister Miller, *Mamisa, The Swazi Warrior* (Pietermaritzburg: Shuter and Shooter, 1933); and Hilda Kuper, *Bite of Hunger* (New York: Harcourt, Brace & World, 1965).

2. Kuper, *Uniform of Colour*, p. 149; Fion de Vletter, "A Socio-Economic Profile of Swazi Rural Homesteads: A Summary of the Main Findings Arising from the Swaziland Homestead Survey" (mimeo, 1982); Margo Russell, "The Rural Homestead in Its Context" (Social Science Research Unit, University of Swaziland, Research Paper No. 3), p. 20. According to Kuper, the average household size in 1947 was 7.2.

3. de Vletter, "Socio-Economic Profile of Swazi Rural Homesteads," pp. 1–3. Other nonagricultural homestead activities listed were selling clothing, hawking produce at markets, hiring out cattle, seasonal agricultural work for neighbors, and truck and tractor hire.

4. Ibid., p. 5.

5. Ibid., p. 10. Virtually all rural homesteads engage in some subsistence agriculture, and two-thirds of them keep cattle.

6. Kuper, *African Aristocracy*, pp. 105–106; Kuper, *The Swazi*, pp. 19–20; Marwick, *The Swazi*, pp. 55–57.

7. Kuper, *The Swazi*, p. 20. To allow Dlamini aristocrats to marry women otherwise prohibited, the Nkosi Dlamini over the years have been divided. The Ginindza and the Mamba, for instance, are offshoots of the original ruling clan.

8. Kuper, *The Swazi*, p. 20; Kuper, *African Aristocracy*, , pp. 110–112.

9. Kuper, *The Swazi*, p. 22.

10. The status of women is the subject of increasing numbers of articles and letters to the press. For instance, "The Legal System Unfair to Women," *Swazi Observer*, 6 March 1982.

11. Kuper, *African Aristocracy*, p. 56.

12. "Swift Revolution in Swaziland Leaves Mystery of Succession," *Washington Post*, 29 April 1983.

13. For a fuller discussion see Kuper, *African Aristocracy*, Chapter 6.

14. Lengthy descriptions may be found in ibid., Chapter 13, and Marwick, *The Swazi*, pp. 182–195. An important study of the cosmology of the ritual, with emphasis on psycholinguistics, is Beidelman, "Swazi Royal Ritual."

15. Kuper, *The Swazi: A South African Kingdom*, pp. 68–71.

16. Ibid., p. 58.

17. Kuper, *The Swazi*, p. 43. See also Kuper, *African Aristocracy*, pp. 186–196.

18. Kuper, *The Swazi: A South African Kingdom*, p. 66. Chapter 1 examines these same insecurities as a basis for the rise in ritual murders in recent years.

19. The Swazi unit of currency is the lilangeni (pl., emalangeni), which means "in the sun."

20. Christopher C. Watts, *Dawn in Swaziland* (London: Society for the Propagation of the Gospel in Foreign Parts, 1922), pp. 35–42.

21. Lord Hailey, *Native Administration in the British African Territories. Part V, The High Commission Territories: Basutoland, the Bechuanaland Protectorate, and Swaziland* (London: H.M.S.O., 1953), p. 336; Swaziland, *Swaziland Census 1956* (n.p., n.d.). After the 1956 census, religious affiliation ceased to be enumerated.

22. Kuper, *The Swazi: A South African Kingdom*, pp. 67–68. In the African context, the word "Zion" in a denomination's title often signifies its posture of separatism, with nationalistic overtones.

23. Since numbers of cattle thereby become the driving economic motive, Swazi owners crowd too many beasts on too little land. Cattle consequently become ill conditioned, and communal grazing land becomes badly eroded. The ultimate harm to the nation's soil is a perennial problem for which the authorities constantly seek solutions—except the obvious (to many) one of reforming the land tenure system.

24. Kuper, *The Swazi: A South African Kingdom*, p. 43.

25. Holleman, *Experiment in Swaziland*, pp. 178 (Table 37), 180 (Table 39), and 193 (Table 58).

26. Swaziland, *Third National Development Plan 1978/79–1982/83* (Mbabane, 1977), p. 181.

27. Ibid. The Cambridge Senior Certificate, the secondary school terminal examination standard throughout much of the former British Empire. Normally students take the "O" (ordinary) level examination; exceptional students attempt the "A" (advanced) level.

28. Swaziland, *Report on the 1976 Swaziland Population Census. Vol. II: Statistical Tables* (Mbabane: Central Statistical Office, 1980).

29. The proposed legislation would also, of course, affect European eligibility for Swazi citizenship. There are currently a number of Europeans who are Swazi citizens.

CHAPTER 3. GOVERNMENT AND POLITICS, 1963–1983

1. Ronald Hyam, *The Failure of South African Expansion 1908–1948* (London: Macmillan, 1972), p. 100. Gwamile herself had been a figure of no little charisma: That she had given no quarter to Europeans of whatever stature is the stuff of a rich Swazi lore. During World War I the mayor of Johannesburg, visiting her, described his recruiting efforts to the war. "If you want recruits for the war, being a big, fat man, why do you not go yourself?" she asked. The mayor changed the subject, mentioning a colleague who was engaged in piping water to town. "When I want water," the queen replied, "I make the rain myself." Christopher C. Watts, *Dawn in Swaziland* (London: Society for the Propagation of the Gospel in Foreign Parts, 1922), p. 35.

2. Martin J. Fransman, "The State and Development in Swaziland, 1962–1977" (Ph.D. dissertation, University of Sussex, 1978), pp. 183–188; J.S.M. Matsebula, *A History of Swaziland* (London: Longman, 1972), pp. 190–195; Hilda Kuper, *Sobhuza II: Ngwenyama and King of Swaziland* (London: Duckworth, 1978), pp. 232–238. In several previous instances, the king had joined interests with the settlers. Controversy was sparked in 1947 when the king exchanged some Swazi Nation Land in the Piggs Peak district for some acreage in the Native Land Settlement Scheme, and several families were forcibly resettled on land they considered inferior. The Piggs Peak tract became the heart of the Peak Timbers Ltd. operations. In 1960 the *ngwenyama* and the settlers both were quick to oppose the pronouncement by the resident commissioner, Brian (later Sir Brian) Marwick, that Swaziland was to become independent under a nonracial, one-man, one-vote constitution. Christian Potholm, *Swaziland: The Dynamics of Political Modernization* (Berkeley: University of California Press, 1972), pp. 48–49. Marwick was resident commissioner from 1957 to 1963 and queen's commissioner until March 1964. He was succeeded by Francis (later Sir Francis) Loyd (1964–1968).

3. Fransman, "State and Development," pp. 145–150, 239–248.

4. Notably the Swaziland Democratic party, led by Simon Sishayi Nxumalo; the Mbandzeni National Convention (Dr. George Msibi); the Swaziland Progressive party (John Nquku); and the Ngwane National Liberatory Congress (Dr. Ambrose Zwane and Prince Dumisa Dlamini).

5. Potholm, *Swaziland*, p. 103.

6. Fransman, "State and Development," pp. 159, 244.

7. Potholm, *Swaziland*, p. 108.

8. Fransman, "State and Development," pp. 277–282.

9. The NNLC drew 20.2 percent of the vote nationally. Fransman, "State and Development," pp. 283–284; Kuper, *Sobhuza II*, pp. 287–289.

10. Potholm, *Swaziland*, p. 1.

11. Colin Legum (ed.), *Africa Contemporary Record 1970–1971* (London: Rex Collings, 1971), p. B542.

12. Colin Legum (ed.), *Africa Contemporary Record 1968–1969* (London: Africa Research Ltd., 1969), p. 356.

13. *Africa Confidential* 13, 9 (5 May 1972):2.

14. Ibid.; Fransman, "State and Development," pp. 294–296.

15. Fransman, "State and Development," p. 295.

16. Ibid., pp. 305–310, 328–334. Quote (R. P. Stephens, 20 April 1973), p. 328. The "outside influences" undoubtedly referred in part to the wave of strikes and violence that had swept Durban during March 1973, the shock of which reached far beyond that port city.

17. The amendment established a five-person tribunal, appointed by the prime minister, to decide cases of "doubtful citizenship." Appeals were to be lodged with him, bypassing the court system. Kuper, *Sobhuza II*, pp. 322–332; Fransman, "State and Development," pp. 324–325.

18. Fransman, "State and Development," p. 326.

19. Ibid., p. 327; Colin Legum (ed.), *Africa Contemporary Record 1973–1974* (London: Rex Collings, 1974), pp. B474–B476.

20. Fransman, "State and Development," pp. 336–337; "Police Arrest Sugar Workers," *Times of Swaziland*, 26 July 1978; "Luphohlo Boycott Continues," *Times of Swaziland*, 10 May 1982.

21. Fransman, "State and Development," pp. 340–341; Colin Legum (ed.), *Africa Contemporary Record 1977–1978* (New York: Africana Publishing Co., 1979), p. B1006.

22. Among those detained for ritual murder in 1981 was the police superintendant Jeremiah Dube, along with three others. He was acquitted.

23. Legum, *Africa Contemporary Record 1973–1974*, p. B476.

24. Colin Legum (ed.), *Africa Contemporary Record 1978–1979* (New York: Africana Publishing Co., 1980), pp. B958–B959; Colin Legum (ed.), *Africa Contemporary Record 1980–1981* (New York: Africana Publishing Co., 1981), pp. B886–B887.

25. Legum, *Africa Contemporary Record 1978–1979*, pp. B958–B959; Colin Legum, (ed.), *Africa Contemporary Record 1979–1980* (New York: Africana Publishing Co., 1981), pp. B926–B927; Legum, *Africa Contemporary Record 1980–1981*, pp. B886–B888; "Swaziland: Corruption Probe Softens," *Africa News* 17, 9 (31 August 1981):9; *Africa Confidential* 21, 16 (30 July 1980):5; *Africa Confidential* 22, 13 (30 July 1981):6–7; *Africa Confidential* 22, 25 (9 December 1981):3.

26. "Beyond Sobhuza," *Sunday Times* (Johannesburg), 29 August 1982.

27. "60 Years and 150 Children Later, Sobhuza II Still Reigns," *Washington Post*, 5 September 1981; "The Lion of Swaziland Celebrates 60 Years as King," *New York Times*, 5 September 1981; "Diamond Jubilee Pictorial," *Times of Swaziland*, September 1981.

28. "The Lion Is Dead, The Elephant Rules," *Rand Daily Mail* (Johannesburg), 3 September 1982; "What Chance for Swazi Democracy?" *Star* (Johannesburg), 18 September 1982; "African Kingdom's Secret: Grooming a New Ruler," *New York Times*, 5 October 1982; "Sons Held in King Poison Probe, *Sunday Times*, 17 October 1982; "Swift Revolution in Swaziland Leaves Mystery of Succession," *Washington Post*, 29 April 1983.

29. "60 Years and 150 Children Later, Sobhuza II Still Reigns."

CHAPTER 4. GEOGRAPHY, RESOURCES, AND THE ECONOMY

1. More extensive geographical, climatological, and natural resource information may be found in the following sources: J. F. Holleman (ed.), *Experiment in Swaziland. Report of the Swaziland Sample Survey 1960 by the Institute of Social Research, University of Natal for the Swaziland Administration* (Cape Town: Oxford University Press, 1964); Swaziland, *Post-Independence Development Plan* (Mbabane, 1969); Swaziland, *Third National Development Plan 1978/79–1982/83* (Mbabane, 1977); T.J.D. Fair, G. Murdoch, and H. M. Jones, *Development in Swaziland: A Regional Analysis* (Johannesburg: Witwatersrand University Press, 1969); Dorothy M. Doveton, *The Human Geography of Swaziland* (London: George Philip & Son, 1937); and Sonya M. Jones, *A Study of Swazi Nutrition: Report of the Swaziland Nutrition Survey 1961–62 for the Swaziland Administration* (Durban: Institute for Social Research, University of Natal, 1963).

2. Population growth rate from Swaziland, *Report on the 1976 Swaziland Population Census. Vol. II: Statistical Tables* (Mbabane: Central Statistical Office, 1980). Other sources quote recent figures as high as 3.4 percent, which appear closer to reality. See Barclays Bank, *Swaziland: An Economic Survey and Businessman's Guide* (Mbabane: Barclays Bank, Ltd., 1981), p. 64.

3. Fair, Murdoch, and Jones, *Development in Swaziland*, pp. 10–11.

4. Swaziland, Central Statistical Office, *Annual Statistical Bulletin 1978* (Mbabane, 1979), p. 20. Cropland as a percentage of total land area has fallen in the past fifteen years. Fair, Murdoch, and Jones (*Development in Swaziland*, p. 16) cite a mid-1960s figure of "more than 20 percent of the area." The *Third National Development Plan*, p. 67, places the percentage at 17.2 percent. The *Annual Statistical Bulletin* figure is 16.6 percent.

5. Swaziland, *Third National Development Plan*, pp. 68–69, outlines the seriousness of the overstocking problem on Swazi Nation Land. Cattle numbers are mutiplying at roughly the rate of population growth, 2.8 percent per year. Current estimates have 525,000 head of cattle and 270,000 sheep and goats grazing on 1,944,677 acres (787,000 ha). Converted to bovine rates this represents a stocking level of 3.95 acres (1.6 ha) per stock unit—the densest rate in Africa. (One stock unit is defined as one adult cattle beast or five small grazing animals). Cattle on Swazi Nation Land contribute little to the national economy.

6. Fair, Murdoch, and Jones, *Development in Swaziland*, p. 16; Swaziland, Central Statistical Office, *Annual Statistical Bulletin 1978*, p. 21.

7. Two rivers have major tributaries. The Mbuluzi is fed by the Mbuluzane. Into the Lusutfu flow the Lusushwana, the Mpuluzi, the Ngwempisi, and the Mkhondvo rivers.

8. Legum, *Africa Contemporary Record 1980–1981*, p. B890. Negotiations of a similar nature with Mozambique have been completed with apparent satisfaction, providing certain percentages of river flows through that country. In early 1983 Swaziland signed an agreement with South Africa and Mozambique to cooperate in planning the use of the waters of common (i.e., the Mlumati, Nkomazi, Lusutfu, Ngwavuma, and Mbuluzi) utilization. "Swaziland Signs Agreement," *Times of Swaziland*, 24 February 1983.

9. Selwyn G. Heilbronn, "Water Law Development and Irrigation in Swaziland, 1910–1980" (Ph.D. dissertation, Cambridge University, 1982), pp. 22–153. A "riparian" water law is one that gives the owner of land abutting banks of

natural streams, by virtue of ownership of such land, preferential rights of water use over those of any others desiring its use. Heilbronn, "Water Laws, Prior Rights, and Government Apportionment of Water in Swaziland, Southern Africa" (mimeo, 1981), suggests that part of the reason for the failure of the government to act is that the "commercial wing of the [Swazi] Nation" (i.e., the Tibiyo Taka Ngwane Fund) has itself become the owner of about 20,000 acres (8,100 ha) of irrigated estate and has substantial equity holdings in other estate companies. It has thus, he argues, developed a considerable economic stake in the status quo.

10. Heilbronn, "Water Laws"; Swaziland, *Second National Development Plan 1973–1977* (Mbabane, 1972), p. 149; Fair, Murdoch, and Jones, *Development in Swaziland*, pp. 16–17; Barclays Bank, *Swaziland: An Economic Survey*, pp. 8–10, 18. Estate irrigation (Tibiyo Taka Ngwane) area on SNL land accounts for 20,000 acres (8,100 ha), smallholdings the remaining 1,500 acres (608 ha). SNL irrigated acreage is to grow to 26,000 acres (10,530 ha) by 1983.

11. Swaziland, *Third National Development Plan*, pp. 169–174.

12. Ibid., pp. 173–174; Barclays Bank, *Swaziland: An Economic Survey*, p. 18; "PM Sets Up Joint Body," *Swazi Observer*, 13 March 1982.

13. John Daniel, "The Political Economy of Colonial and Post-Colonial Swaziland," *South African Labour Bulletin* 7, 6 (April 1982):94.

14. Ibid.; Barclays Bank, *Swaziland: An Economic Survey*, pp. 22–23.

15. Fair, Murdoch, and Jones, *Development in Swaziland*, especially Chapters 1, 6, 9, 10, and 11; Barclays Bank, *Swaziland: An Economic Survey*, p. 6; Swaziland, *Third National Development Plan*, p. 65.

16. Percentage figures from Swaziland, *Third National Development Plan*, pp. 6, 65. Barclays Bank, *Swaziland: An Economic Survey*, p. 6, attributes 56 percent to SNL and 44 percent to ITFs.

17. Barclays Bank, *Swaziland: An Economic Survey*, pp. 6–7; Swaziland, *Third National Development Plan*, p. 65; Swaziland, Prime Minister's Office, Department of Economic Planning and Statistics, "Economic Review 1978–1981" (Mbabane, 1982, mimeo), pp. 9, 22.

18. Wage patterns for female agricultural workers and their social consequences are discussed in Patricia McFadden, "Women in Wage-Labour in Swaziland: A Focus on Agriculture," *South African Labour Bulletin* 7, 6 (April 1982):140–166.

19. Swaziland, *Third National Development Plan*, pp. 71, 169–171; Barclays Bank, *Swaziland: An Economic Survey*, pp. 6–7; Daniel, "Political Economy of Swaziland," pp. 103–105. The Third Development Plan called for a total national capital expenditure budget of E 69,378,000 during 1980-1981. On 30 April 1980, Tibiyo declared its accumulated funds to amount to E 37,963,216. As reported by Barclays Bank, Tibiyo's income for 1978-1979 was E 9.4 million, of which E 9.3 million was from dividends. The lilangeni (pl. emalangeni, "E"), the Swazi currency unit, is pegged to the South African unit of currency, the rand. In July 1980 the lilangeni equaled roughly $1.34; in July 1982, $.87; in January 1983, $.95.

20. Swaziland, *Second National Development Plan*, pp. 30–33; Martin J. Fransman, "The State and Development in Swaziland, 1960–1977" (Ph.D. Dissertation, University of Sussex, 1978), pp. 313–315.

21. Lord Hailey, *Native Administration in the British African Territories. Part V, The High Commission Territories: Basutoland, the Bechuanaland Protectorate, and Swaziland* (London: H.M.S.O., 1953), pp. 417–418.

22. Swaziland, *Third National Development Plan*, p. 77; Fion de Vletter, "Subsistence Farmer, Cash Cropper, or Consumer?: A Socio-Economic Profile of a

Sample of Swazi Rural Homesteads" (Mbabane, Ministry of Agriculture, 1979, mimeo), pp. 7–10.

23. de Vletter, "Subsistence Farmer," pp. 72–76; Fion de Vletter. "The Swazi Rural Homestead: Preliminary Findings of a Socio-Economic Survey Undertaken Jointly by the United States Agency for International Development (USAID) and the University College of Swaziland" (mimeo, 1981); A.R.C. Low, "Migration and Agricultural Development in Swaziland: A Micro-Economic Analysis" (Geneva: International Labour Organisation, 1977, mimeo).

24. de Vletter, "Subsistence Farmer," pp. 72–76; Fransman, "State and Development," pp. 311–322.

25. Swaziland, Prime Minister's Office, Department of Economic Planning and Statistics, "Economic Review 1978–1981," pp. 9, 21.

26. Daniel, "Political Economy of Swaziland," pp. 108–109; Barclays Bank, *Swaziland: An Economic Survey*, pp. 8–11.

27. Swaziland, *Third National Development Plan*, pp. 74, 80. Wattle is ideal for local use, being the fastest growing and most productive wood per unit of labor and of land. As a tree crop it can be used for building and for firewood, and it can be sold as charcoal or to tanning extract factories.

28. Information on the following agricultural exports is derived from Barclays Bank, *Swaziland: An Economic Survey*, pp. 11–15.

29. Ibid., pp. 11–15; Swaziland, *Third National Development Plan*, p. 99.

30. Swaziland, *Third National Development Plan*, pp. 95–96, 99–101; Barclays Bank, *Swaziland: An Economic Survey*, p. 34.

31. National Industrial Development Corporation of Swaziland, "A Guide for Investors in Swaziland" (Mbabane, 1980), cited in Daniel, "Political Economy of Swaziland," 102. See also Barclays Bank, *Swaziland: An Economic Survey*, pp. 37–38.

32. Swaziland, *Third National Development Plan*, p. 44.

33. Donald K. Kowet, *Land, Labour Migration and Politics in Southern Africa: Botswana, Lesotho and Swaziland* (Uppsala: Scandinavian Institute of African Studies, 1978), pp. 117–118, 140. South Africa's violation of the "free interchange of goods" provision has historical roots in its barring Swazi cattle from its market from 1924 until the war on "veterinary" grounds by imposing weight restrictions. Swaziland learned that lesson well. In 1980 it closed off imports of South African fruits and vegetables during the Republic's cholera epidemic. One result was the fostering of a vigorous market for locally produced fruits and vegetables, and the "cholera" restrictions remain.

34. Swaziland, Prime Minister's Office, Department of Economic Planning and Statistics, "Economic Review 1978–1981," p. 3.

35. Daniel, "Political Economy of Swaziland," pp. 100–102. Kirsh, now one of South Africa's richest men, got his start in Swaziland in 1958 by obtaining the monopoly for the milling of all maize grown or imported into the kingdom.

36. Tibiyo Taka Ngwane, *A Nation in Progress* (Swaziland: ABC Press, 1978); Barclays Bank, *Swaziland: An Economic Survey*, p. 35; Fransman, "State and Development," pp. 288–292; Daniel, "Political Economy of Swaziland," pp. 103–105.

37. "Swaziland's Venture on the High Seas Gets in Deep Water," *Wall Street Journal*, 31 August 1979.

38. Daniel, "Political Economy of Swaziland," pp. 103–104.

39. Tibiyo Taka Ngwane, *A Nation in Progress*.

40. *Times of Swaziland*, 10 January 1976, cited in Fransman, "State and Development," p. 288.

41. It is referred to as the "Swazi Nation," on p. 101 of the plan.
42. Tibiyo Taka Ngwane, *A Nation in Progress*; Fransman, "State and Development," p. 290.
43. Daniel, "Political Economy of Swaziland," p. 105.
44. The classic study of neocolonialism in Africa and its effects, in a voluminous and growing literature, remains Colin Leys's *Underdevelopment in Kenya: The Political Economy of Neo-Colonialism 1964–1971* (London: Heinemann, 1975).

CHAPTER 5. SWAZILAND'S INTERNATIONAL RELATIONS

1. Swaziland maintains diplomatic relations with a number of countries, including Botswana, Canada, Chile, Egypt, France, Guinea, India, Iran, Israel, Japan, Kenya, Lesotho, Mozambique, Portugal, the Republic of China (Taiwan), South Korea, Spain, Tanzania, the United Kingdom, the United States, West Germany, and Zambia. Colin Legum, ed., *Africa Contemporary Record*, years 1968–1969 to 1980–1981, passim. Swaziland's relations with Mozambique include an agreement to involuntarily repatriate refugees from each other, which is in disregard of the United Nations Refugee Convention. In mid-1980 Swazi authorities detained about ninety Mozambican refugees, but whether they were handed over to Maputo was not known. Richard F. Weisfelder, "Human Rights Under Majority Rule in Southern Africa: The Mote in Thy Brother's Eye," mimeo, p. 45; to be published in Claude E. Welch, Jr., and Ronald I. Meltzer (eds.), *Human Rights and Development in Africa: Domestic Regional and International Dilemmas* (Albany: State University of New York Press, forthcoming); Colin Legum (ed.), *Africa Contemporary Record 1980–1981* (New York: Africana Publishing Co., 1981), p. B890.
2. Legum, *Africa Contemporary Record 1980–1981*, p. B890. In 1982 EEC meat inspectors barred Swaziland's exports from that market until sanitary conditions in its abattoirs were improved.
3. The *South African Labour Bulletin* 7, 6 ("Focus on Swaziland," April 1982) brings together much of the most recent scholarship on the subject. It contains the following articles: Alan Booth, "The Development of the Swazi Labour Market 1900–1968," pp. 34–57; Martin Fransman, "Labour, Capital and the State in Swaziland, 1962–1977," pp. 58–89; John Daniel, "The Political Economy of Colonial and Post-Colonial Swaziland," pp. 90–113; Fion de Vletter, "Labour Migration in Swaziland: Recent Trends and Implications," pp. 114–139; and Patricia McFadden, "Women in Wage-Labour in Swaziland: A Focus on Agriculture," pp. 140–166. See also Donald K. Kowet, *Land, Labour Migration and Politics in Southern Africa: Botswana, Lesotho and Swaziland* (Uppsala: Scandinavian Institute of African Studies, 1978), pp. 85–110; and Fion de Vletter, "Migrant Labour in Swaziland: Characteristics, Attitudes and Policy Implications" (Geneva: International Labour Organisation, 1978). The best recent comprehensive account of migrant labor and its changing role in South Africa is Merle Lipton, "Men of Two Worlds: Migrant Labour in South Africa," *Optima* 29 (1980):72–201.
4. Booth, "Swazi Labour Market," pp. 45–46.
5. King Sobhuza's address to Parliament, 16 February 1982, cited in Daniel, "Political Economy of Swaziland," p. 109. Swazi labor migrants to South Africa's gold mines numbered 11,297 in 1979 and 9,367 in 1980. Figures from The Employment Bureau of Africa office, Mbabane.
6. For instance, the achievement of power by the Front for the Liberation of Mozambique (FRELIMO) government (1975) in Mozambique, which under the Portuguese had been a major supplier of labor. The new government announced

its intention to reduce, and ultimately eliminate, its quota. In 1982 Mozambique, like the other countries in the region, was again dispatching as many migrant laborers as South Africa would accept.

7. Fion de Vletter, personal communication, 8 October 1982.

8. For a more detailed discussion of these issues see Kowet, *Land, Labour Migration and Politics in Southern Africa*, pp. 111–144.

9. Richard F. Weisfelder, "The Southern African Development Coordination Conference (SADCC): A New Factor in the Liberation Process," mimeo, p. 26; to be published in Thomas M. Callaghy (ed.), *South Africa in Southern Africa* (New York: Praeger Publishers, forthcoming).

10. Legum, *Africa Contemporary Record 1980–1981*, pp. A24–A30.

11. Weisfelder, "SADCC," p. 9; Douglas C. Anglin, "SADCC *versus* PTA: Competitive or Complementary Approaches to Economic Liberation and Regional Cooperation in Southern Africa" (paper presented at the African Studies Association Conference, November 1982), mimeo, p. 6.

12. Barclays Bank, *Swaziland: An Economic Survey and Businessman's Guide* (Mbabane: Barclays Bank Ltd., 1981), p. 41; Daniel, "Political Economy of Swaziland," p. 101. For a description of the Richards Bay development, including its impressive technology, see "Coal's Surge as a South African Export," *New York Times*, 24 March 1982.

13. The BLS countries are further constrained within SADCC by their obligation under terms of the customs union to obtain South Africa's approval before entering into outside trade agreements. Anglin, "SADCC *versus* PTA," p. 12.

14. The *New York Times* follows these issues consistently. See, for instance: "Along Zimbabwe's Border, a War Is Still Going On," 4 October 1981; "In South Africa, Drought Turns Dreams to Dust," 26 May 1982. See also "S. African Railroads Bind African Economy," *Washington Star*, 18 July 1981; "The View from Inside the Laager," *Financial Times* (London), 1 September 1981.

15. James North, "King Sobhuza's Limos," *New Republic*, 20 September 1980, p. 15. See also Legum, *Africa Contemporary Record 1980–1981*, pp. B892–B893.

16. Two incidents in late 1981 demonstrated the cavalier way South Africa violated the sanctity of Swaziland's borders. In November an armed group of South African mercenaries, identifying themselves as a rugby team, entered Swaziland by bus and flew on a scheduled Royal Swazi airliner to the Seychelles, where they staged a bloody but unsuccessful attempt to overthrow its government. The aircraft was destroyed, although innocent crew and passengers emerged unscathed, at least physically. In December an automobile containing two men, a Swazi national and a South African refugee, was ambushed several hundred yards inside Swaziland by South Africans using automatic weapons. The two men were killed and the car destroyed. Apparently the vehicle contained weapons and was about to cross into South Africa clandestinely on an ANC mission. In both cases the Swazi government's official reaction was extraordinarily subdued.

17. Legum, *Africa Contemporary Record 1980–1981*, p. B889.

18. Allister Sparks, "Why Botha Wants to Give Territory to King Sobhuza," *Observer*, 9 May 1982.

19. "Swaziland Being Duped," *Star* (Johannesburg, weekly airmail edition), 17 July 1982.

20. "South Africa Would Yield 'Homeland' to Neighbor," *New York Times*, 3 March 1982; "South Africa Tells Tribe of Transfer," *New York Times*, 18 June

1982; Sparks, "Why Botha Wants to Give Territory to King Sobhuza"; "South Africa's Swaziland Scheme," *Christian Science Monitor*, 23 June 1982.

21. "The Big Land Swap Flop," *Star* (weekly airmail edition), 9 October 1982; "South Africa Concedes Defeat in Move to Cede Area to Swaziland," *Washington Post*, 26 November 1982.

CHAPTER 6. THE PRESSURES OF MODERNITY

1. For the Swazi version of the argument see J.S.M. Matsebula, *A History of Swaziland* (London: Longman, 1972), pp. 40–42, 87–114. See also Philip L. Bonner, "The Rise, Consolidation, and Disintegration of Dlamini Power in Swaziland Between 1820 and 1889. A Study in the Relationship Between Foreign Affairs and Internal Political Development" (Ph.D. dissertation, University of London, 1977), pp. 326–335, 345–352, 373–378, and 397–401.

2. The Zulu were not considered entirely removed as a threat by the Swazi until Cetewayo's defeat by the British at Ulundi in 1879.

3. Swaziland, *Maize in Swaziland: A Review of Its Production and Marketing in Recent Years* (Mbabane: Ministry of Agriculture and Cooperatives, 1980), pp. 39–40; Fion de Vletter, "Subsistence Farmer, Cash Cropper, or Consumer?: A Socio-Economic Profile of a Sample of Swazi Rural Homesteads" (Mbabane: Ministry of Agriculture, 1979, mimeo), p. 59.

4. Swaziland, *Maize in Swaziland*, p. 56.

5. Swaziland, *Third National Development Plan 1978/79–1982/83* (Mbabane, 1977), p. 99; Swaziland, *Establishment of a Third Sugar Factory and Plantation. Final Planning and Development Study. Volume I: Main Report* (Bromley: Tate & Lyle Technical Services Ltd., 1975), pp. 76–78. The report observes: "The dilemma of many developing and developed countries is that increases in productivity through mechanization may cause unemployment and hence be socially inacceptable. Swaziland is not in this position" (p. 77).

6. "Swaziland: The Frustrated Inquiry," *Africa Confidential* 22, 13 (July 1981): 6–7; "Swaziland: Corruption Probe Softens," *Africa News* 17, 9 (August 31, 1981):9.

7. It is ironic that in the early 1980s Swaziland, professing to be in the vanguard of the struggle for human rights in southern Africa, was still denying equality of opportunity to a segment of its citizenry. The Eurafricans ("coloureds") had for the most part been denied the basic political rights of Swazi citizenship by the government since independence (see pp. 60–61).

8. "African Kingdom's Secret: Grooming a New Ruler," *New York Times*, 5 October 1982; "Boy Groomed to Be King," *Columbus* (Ohio) *Citizen-Journal*, 5 January 1983; "Boy King Goes to School in England," *Sunday Times* (Johannesburg), 6 February 1983; "Swift Revolution in Swaziland Leaves Mystery of Succession," *Washington Post*, 29 April 1983. The English public school selected for the crown prince's education was Sherborne, in Dorset.

9. "Power Struggles Rock Swazi Cabinet," *Star* (Johannesburg), 16 February 1983; "Liqoqo Members Accused of Seditious Statements: Mfanasibili and Chief in Court," *Times of Swaziland*, 8 March 1983; "Swazi PM Axed in Palace Coup," *Rand Daily Mail* (Johannesburg), 22 March 1983; "Bhekimpi Named PM," *Times of Swaziland*, 24 March 1983; "Plummet of a Popular Prince," *Star* (Johannesburg; airmail edition), 2 April 1983; "The Current Political Situation in Swaziland" (Maputo: Centro de Estudos Africanos, Universidade Eduardo Mondlane, 1983), p.

4; John Daniel, "The South African-Swazi State Relationship: Ideological Harmony and Structural Domination" (mimeo, 1983), pp. 4–5.

10. "New King Named," *Times of Swaziland*, 11 August 1983.

11. Colin Leys, *Underdevelopment in Kenya: The Political Economy of Neo-colonialism 1964–1971* (London: Heinemann, 1975), pp. 1–27, 254–258.

12. Ibid., p. 27.

Abbreviations

ANC	African National Congress
BLS	Botswana, Lesotho, and Swaziland
CDC	Commonwealth Development Corporation
EEC	European Economic Community
GDP	gross domestic product
INM	Imbokodvo National Movement
ITF	individual tenure farms
MNR	National Resistance Movement (Mozambique)
MP	member of Parliament
NIDCS	National Industrial Development Corporation of Swaziland
NNLC	Ngwane National Liberatory Congress
NRC	Native Recruiting Corporation
OAU	Organization of African Unity
PAC	Pan-Africanist Congress
RDA	Rural Development Areas
SADCC	Southern African Development Coordination Conference
SEDCO	Small Enterprises Development Company
SNL	Swazi Nation Land
USA	United Swaziland Association

Bibliography

Barclays Bank. *Swaziland: An Economic Survey and Businessman's Guide.* Mbabane: Barclays Bank Ltd., 1981.

Beidelman, T. O. "Swazi Royal Ritual." *Africa* 36, 4 (1966):373–405.

Bonner, Philip L. "Classes, the Mode of Production and the State in Pre-Colonial Swaziland." In *Economy and Society in Pre-Industrial South Africa,* edited by Anthony Atmore and Shula Marks. London: Longman, 1980.

————. "The Rise, Consolidation, and Disintegration of Dlamini Power in Swaziland Between 1820 and 1889. A Study in the Relationship Between Foreign Affairs and Internal Political Development." Ph.D. dissertation, University of London, 1977.

————. *Kings, Commoners and Concessionaires: The Evolution and Dissolution of the Nineteenth-Century Swazi State.* Cambridge: Cambridge University Press, 1983.

Booth, Alan. "The Development of the Swazi Labour Market 1900–1968." *South African Labour Bulletin* 7, 6 (April 1982):34–57.

Bryant, A. T. *Olden Times in Zululand and Natal.* London: Longmans Green, 1929.

Crush, Jonathan S. "The Colonial Division of Space: The Significance of the Swaziland Land Partition," *International Journal of African Historical Studies* 13, 1 (1980):71–86.

————. "The Genesis of Colonial Land Policy in Swaziland." *South African Geographical Journal* 62, 1 (1980):73–88.

————. "The Parameters of Dependence in Southern Africa: A Case Study of Swaziland." *Journal of Southern African Affairs* 4, 1 (January 1979):55–66.

————. "Settler Estate Production, Monopoly Control, and the Imperial Response: The Case of the Swaziland Corporation Ltd." *African Economic History* 8 (Fall 1979):183–198.

Daniel, John. "The Political Economy of Colonial and Post-Colonial Swaziland." *South African Labour Bulletin* 7, 6 (April 1982):90–113.

de Vletter, Fion. "Labour Migration in Swaziland: Recent Trends and Implications." *South African Labour Bulletin* 7, 6 (April 1982):114–139.

————. "Subsistence Farmer, Cash Cropper, or Consumer?: A Socio-Economic Profile of a Sample of Swazi Rural Homesteads." Mbabane: Ministry of Agriculture, 1979 (mimeo).

Doveton, Dorothy M. *The Human Geography of Swaziland.* London: George Philip & Son, 1937.

149

Doxey, G. V. *The High Commission Territories and the Republic of South Africa.* London: Oxford University Press, 1963.

Fair, T.J.D., Murdoch, G., and Jones, H. M. *Development in Swaziland: A Regional Analysis.* Johannesburg: Witwatersrand University Press, 1969.

Forbes, David. *My Life in South Africa.* London: Witherby, 1938.

Fransman, Martin J. "Labour, Capital and the State in Swaziland, 1962–1977." *South African Labour Bulletin* 7, 6 (April 1982):58–89.

_____. "The State and Development in Swaziland, 1960–1977." Ph.D. dissertation, University of Sussex, 1978.

Garson, Noel. *The Swaziland Question and the Road to the Sea, 1887–1895.* Pp. 271–422 in A. Kisser et al., *Archives Year Book for South African History,* Vol. II. Parow: Cape Times, 1957.

Great Britain. *Financial and Economic Situation of Swaziland. Report of the Commission Appointed by the Secretary of State for Dominion Affairs, January 1932.* London: His Majesty's Stationery Office, 1932. (The Pim Report, Cmd. 4114).

Hailey, Lord. *Native Administration in the British African Territories. Part V, The High Commission Territories: Basutoland, the Bechuanaland Protectorate, and Swaziland.* London: Her Majesty's Stationery Office, 1953.

_____. *The Republic of South Africa and the High Commission Territories.* London: Oxford University Press, 1963.

Halpern, Jack. *South Africa's Hostages: Basutoland, Bechuanaland, and Swaziland.* Baltimore: Penguin Books, 1965.

Heilbronn, Selwyn G. "Water Law Development and Irrigation in Swaziland, 1910–1980." Ph.D. dissertation, Cambridge University, 1982.

_____. "Water Laws, Prior Rights, and Government Apportionment of Water in Swaziland, Southern Africa." Mimeo, 1981. (Obtainable from the Social Science Research Unit, University of Swaziland, Kwaluseni).

Holleman, J. F. (ed.). *Experiment in Swaziland. Report of the Swaziland Sample Survey 1960 by the Institute of Social Research, University of Natal for the Swaziland Administration.* Cape Town: Oxford University Press, 1964.

Hughes, A.J.B. *Swazi Land Tenure.* Durban: Institute for Social Research, University of Natal, 1964.

Hyam, Ronald. *The Failure of South African Expansion 1908–1948.* London: Macmillan, 1972.

International Bank for Reconstruction and Development. *1978 World Bank Atlas.* Washington, D.C.: World Bank, 1978.

International Labour Organisation. *Reducing Dependence: A Strategy for Productive Employment and Development in Swaziland.* Addis Ababa: International Labour Office, Jobs and Skills Programme for Africa, 1977.

Jones, Sonya M. *A Study of Swazi Nutrition: Report of the Swaziland Nutrition Survey 1961–62 for the Swaziland Administration.* Durban: Institute for Social Research, University of Natal, 1963.

Kowet, Donald K. *Land, Labour Migration and Politics in Southern Africa: Botswana, Lesotho and Swaziland.* Uppsala: Scandinavian Institute of African Studies, 1978.

Kuper, Hilda. *An African Aristocracy: Rank Among the Swazi.* London: Oxford University Press, 1947; reprinted 1980.

_____. *Sobhuza II: Ngwenyama and King of Swaziland.* London: Duckworth, 1978.

_____. *The Swazi.* London: International African Institute, 1952.

_____. *The Swazi: A South African Kingdom.* New York: Holt, Rinehart and Winston, 1963.

_____ . *The Uniform of Colour: A Study of White-Black Relationships in Swaziland.* Johannesburg: Witwatersrand University Press, 1947.

Landell-Mills, P. M. "The 1969 Southern African Customs Union Agreement." *Journal of Modern African Studies* 9, 2 (1971):262–281.

Leistner, G.M.E., and Smit, P. *Swaziland: Resources and Development.* Pretoria: African Institute of South Africa, 1969.

Leys, Colin. *Underdevelopment in Kenya: The Political Economy of Neo-Colonialism 1964–1971.* London: Heinemann, 1975.

Lipton, Merle. "Men of Two Worlds: Migrant Labour in South Africa." *Optima* 29 (1980):72–201.

McFadden, Patricia. "Women in Wage-Labour in Swaziland: A Focus on Agriculture." *South African Labour Bulletin* 7, 6 (April 1982):140–166.

Marwick, Brian A. *The Swazi: An Ethnographic Account of the Natives of the Swaziland Protectorate.* Cambridge: Cambridge University Press, 1940.

Mashasha, Francis J. "The Road to Colonialism: Concessions and the Collapse of Swazi Independence, 1875–1926." Ph.D. dissertation, Oxford University, 1977.

Matsebula. J.S.M. *A History of Swaziland.* London: Longman, 1972.

Myburgh, A. C. *The Tribes of the Barberton District.* Pretoria: Union of South Africa, Department of Native Affairs (Ethnological Publications No. 25), 1949.

Nyeko, Balam. "The Swazi Leadership's Response to Colonial Rule, 1902–1930." Ph.D. dissertation, Makerere University, 1977.

Omer-Cooper, J. D. *The Zulu Aftermath.* Evanston, Ill.: Northwestern University Press, 1966.

Perham, Margery, and Curtis, Lionel. *The Protectorates of South Africa.* London: Oxford University Press, 1935.

Potholm, Christian. *Swaziland: The Dynamics of Political Modernization.* Berkeley: University of California Press, 1972.

Stevens, Richard P. *Lesotho, Botswana, and Swaziland: The Former High Commission Territories in Southern Africa.* New York: Praeger Publishers, 1967.

Swaziland. *Maize in Swaziland: A Review of Its Production and Marketing in Recent Years.* Mbabane: Ministry of Agriculture and Cooperatives, 1980.

_____ . *Post-Independence Development Plan.* Mbabane, 1969.

_____ . *Second National Development Plan 1973–1977.* Mbabane, 1972.

_____ . *Third National Development Plan 1978/79–1982/83.* Mbabane, 1977.

Tibiyo Taka Ngwane. *A Nation in Progress.* Swaziland: ABC Press, 1978.

Watts, Christopher C. *Dawn in Swaziland.* London: Society for the Propagation of the Gospel in Foreign Parts, 1922.

Wilson, Monica, and Thompson, Leonard (eds.). *The Oxford History of South Africa. Volume II: South Africa, 1870–1966.* London: Oxford University Press, 1971.

Youé, C. P. "Imperial Land Policy in Swaziland and the African Response." *Journal of Imperial and Commonwealth History* 7, 1 (1978):56–70.

Index

152

and marriage, 11, 39, 43, 46, 49, 54.
  See also Polygyny
and the Middle East, 96, 97
mineral resources of, 2, 13, 16, 17, 20,
  23, 65, 66, 89–90, 105, 106. *See also*
  individual minerals
and mining, 2, 4, 13, 17, 19, 20, 23,
  24, 31, 32, 89–90, 110–111
and Mozambique, 1, 7, 12, 32, 98, 108,
  113, 115, 117–118, 120, 124, 129
population, 21, 27, 31, 32, 35, 58, 81,
  83, 84, 92, 109(table)
population/land ratio, 23
and Pretoria, 118, 119, 121, 124, 125,
  129
railroad, 26, 75, 81, 90, 114, 116
and religion, 48–49, 50, 50(table), 51,
  51(table). *See also* Medicine men;
  Rainmaking; Sorcery; Witchcraft;
  Zionism
rivers in, 83, 86–87, 88
road system, 26
and South Africa, 1, 4, 17, 19, 20, 23,
  24, 26, 32, 55, 63, 70, 71, 74, 81, 96,
  97, 98, 102, 103, 105, 108, 109, 110,
  111–116, 122, 124–125, 128–129, 130
taxation, 2, 4, 16–17, 19, 23, 26, 27,
  95, 103, 107, 135–136(n35, n36)
topography of, 81–82, 85
and Transvaal, 1, 7, 10, 11, 12, 15–16,
  17, 19, 21, 24, 27, 32, 89, 114, 118,
  123–124
and the United Nations, 108, 116, 118
and the United States, 95, 105, 108,
  116, 130
and Zimbabwe, 10, 113, 115, 124
Swazi National Council, 63, 66
Swazi Nation Land (SNL), 65, 66, 70, 71,
  87–88, 91, 92, 94, 95
Swazi Observer, 106

Tangoma. *See* Diviners
Tenant labor, 24, 27. *See also* Migrant
  labor
Thandile (queen mother), 45
Tibiyo Taka Ngwane Fund, 5, 62, 70, 77,
  89, 91, 92, 95, 96, 105–107, 126, 127
Timber, 2, 31, 32, 95–96, 105. *See also*
  Forestry, commercial
Times of Swaziland, 21, 106
Tin, 2, 13, 24, 89, 90
Tinyanga. See Medicine men
Tisuka Taka Ngwane Fund, 106, 127

Tobacco, 24, 27, 83, 92, 93(table), 94, 97,
  99(table)
Todd, Carl, 67
Tourism, 31, 101–102, 106, 137(n55)
Traditionalism, 34, 42, 43, 47, 62, 65, 68,
  75, 79, 122, 125, 128
in agriculture, 91, 92
in religion, 50–51
Transvaal. *See* Swaziland, and Transvaal
Trypanosomiasis, 8

Umhlanga (Reed Dance) ceremony,
  42(photo), 43
Unallotted Lands Concession, 30
Underdevelopment, 21
"Underdevelopment theory," 4
Underproductivity, 54, 126, 127
Unemployment, 2, 3, 110–111, 127
Unions, 32, 67, 72, 74
United Kingdom. *See* Swaziland, and
  Great Britain
United Nations. *See* Swaziland, and the
  United Nations
United States. *See* Swaziland, and the
  United States
United Swaziland Association (USA),
  66–69
University of Swaziland, 56(photo), 57
Urbanization, 34, 43
Urban migration, 55, 72
USA. *See* United Swaziland Association

Voting. *See* Elections
Vuvulane, 126

Water rights, 87
Wealth, distribution of, 53–54, 61–62
Witchcraft, 49–50
Witwatersrand, 16, 17
Women, 8, 34, 35, 42–43, 44(fig.), 52, 53,
  54. *See also* Polygyny; Swaziland,
  marriage
Working class, 65, 75
World War I, 19, 29
World War II, 31, 42, 63

Xhosa, 7

Zambezi, 19
Zimbabwe. *See* Swaziland, and Zimbabwe
Zionism, 51
Zulu, 1, 7, 10, 11, 12, 19, 27, 119, 124,
  134(n9)
Zululand, 17
Zulu wars (of expansionism), 1, 8
Zwane, Ambrose, 70, 73